TRAVELLERS

PRAGUE

By
LOUIS JAMES

Written by Louis James, updated by Marc Di Duca
Original photography by Jon Wyand

Published by Thomas Cook Publishing
A division of Thomas Cook Tour Operations Limited.
Company registration no. 1450464 England
The Thomas Cook Business Park, Unit 9, Coningsby Road,
Peterborough PE3 8SB, United Kingdom
Email: books@thomascook.com, Tel: + 44 (0) 1733 416477
www.thomascookpublishing.com

Produced by Cambridge Publishing Management Limited
Burr Elm Court, Main Street, Caldecote CB23 7NU

ISBN: 978-1-84848-006-3

Series Editor: Maisie Fitzpatrick
Production/DTP: Steven Collins

Printed and bound in Italy by Printer Trento

Cover photography: Front: L–R: Robert Harding Picture Library/Alamy;
© FAN Travelstock/Alamy; © Picture Finders/Pictures Colour Library.
Back: © Picture Finders/Pictures Colour Library

Contents

KEY TO MAPS

▲ Mountain
♣ Park
✈ Airport
ⓘ Information
🕆 Church
🏛 Museum
★ Start of walk
Ⓢ Bank
Railway line

╲ Ancient walls
— Motorway
═ Main road
⋯ Minor road
— Railway
⋯ Ferry route
Ⓜ Metro station
Fountain

Introduction

The 'Golden City', the 'City of a Hundred Spires', the 'Paris of the Thirties': Prague (Praha) has inspired any number of flattering and romantic descriptions. It wears such laurels lightly, since its mixture of beauty and an atmosphere soaked in history speaks for itself.

Prague, it is often said, lies at the heart of Europe. Under its first ruling dynasty, the Přemyslids, and still more under the first three Luxembourg kings of Bohemia (1310–1419), it rose to be the focus of a great Central European empire. It reached its apogee of wealth and splendour under Charles IV (1346–78), who was also elected Holy Roman Emperor. All this began to fall apart when the violent religious struggles of the 15th century between the followers of the reformer Jan Hus and Catholic rulers split the country.

The Hussite wars also sharpened the age-old conflict between Germans (occupying many of the most influential offices of Church and State) and native Slavs. In fact, Prague had been a twin-cultured city, Slavic and Germanic, ever since Otakar II invited Germans to colonise the left bank of the River Vltava in 1257. It remained so up to the 20th century, with German domination being the basis of the Habsburg rule between 1526 and 1918.

A third, deeply influential cultural element was supplied by the Jews who, though they number only about 2,000 today, formed 25 per cent of the city's population in 1700.

Finally, the Roma (gypsy) minority, although still largely ignored, has always been an important part of the city's population. Recognition of their place in society was a precondition to

Mosaic in the Emmaus Monastery (Klášter Emauzy)

the Czech Republic's acceptance into the European Union.

Despite being washed over by so many conflicts – dynastic, religious, racial – Prague has remained one of the world's best-preserved cities. Here, as nowhere else, you can sip a beer in one of dozens of Romanesque and Gothic cellars, wander around some of the finest Gothic and Baroque churches in Europe, or track down unique exotic examples of Art Nouveau or Cubist architecture. The people of Prague, having lived through wars and oppression, have earned a reputation for resourcefulness on the one hand,

and resilience and doggedness on the other. The hero of the novel *The Good Soldier Švejk* represents the former quality; playwright and statesman Václav Havel, with his determination to 'live in truth', embodies the latter.

Prague today has come alive after 40 years of Communist gloom. Over a decade and a half after the 'changes', the city has been transformed. Its marvellous musical tradition continues, artistic and cultural activity is as vibrant as ever, and its hundreds of beautiful buildings and impressive monuments have been renovated.

Surrounded by history in Old Town Square (Staré Město)

The city

Prague lies 50 degrees 5 minutes north, and 14 degrees 25 minutes east – a city at the centre of Europe, but part of both Western and Eastern European culture.

Its topography is determined by the River Vltava. The 497sq km (192sq mile) conurbation stretches 48km (30 miles) along both banks of the river, a huge expansion from the modest town of 1883 (8.5sq km/3¹/₄sq miles).

Like Rome, Prague is built on seven hills. On the left (western) bank of the Vltava, the wedge-shaped plateau called Hradčany rises abruptly from a narrow ribbon of land along the shore. One of the four great cities of Central Europe (the others being Budapest, Kraków and Vienna), Prague lay on important trade routes from Germany, Poland, Russia and the East.

The toll levied on the Judith Bridge across the Vltava brought in revenue for the Crown: the town benefited from the supply of goods and services. The construction of the Charles Bridge in 1357 was a practical necessity, since flood waters had all but swept away its predecessor. While the original inhabitants of Prague had chosen the better-protected slopes above the west bank for their dwellings, flooding on the east side continued until the late 13th century. The problem was partially solved by raising the street level in Staré Město (Old Town). Systematic regulation of the Vltava had to wait until the 19th century.

Areas of Prague

The Czech-Austrian journalist Barbara Condenhove-Kalergi wrote that 'Prague is actually composed of two parts. On the right bank of the Vltava is the Old Town – the Prague of Franz Kafka, the Prague of the Jewish community, the Prague of the Hussites, Czech Prague.

To the left of the Vltava is the Lesser Quarter – the Baroque, the Catholic Prague, the Prague of the Counter-Reformation with its palaces of the nobility, with its many churches and monasteries.'

THOMAS COOK'S PRAGUE

When the state of Czechoslovakia was created after World War I, Thomas Cook began actively to promote tours to Prague and the surrounding countryside. In 1922 the *Thomas Cook Travellers Gazette*, founded in 1851, carried an article promoting the spas and health resorts of Czechoslovakia and describing Prague as one of the most attractive cities on the Continent.

The city is a study in architectural styles

It was only in 1784 that the Emperor Joseph II ordered the four historic towns of Prague – Hradčany and Malá Strana (the Lesser Quarter) on the west bank of the Vltava, and Staré Město and Nové Město (the Old and New Towns) on the east bank – to be merged into a single municipality. Josefov, the Jewish ghetto, was amalgamated with Staré Město in 1850. Except for a large slice of Nové Město, these historic areas today constitute Prague's First District.

Most of historic Prague, and, therefore, most tourist sights, are located in Praha 1. The modern capital now has 22 districts, the result of expansion over the last two centuries and the recent inclusion of several satellite towns.

Climate

Prague's climate is dictated by oceanic and continental influences. The average temperature of 9°C (48°F) implies a mild climate, but it can be very hot in summer (May–September), while in winter (November–March) the temperature stays at or drops well below zero.

The famous Café Slavia is a good meeting place

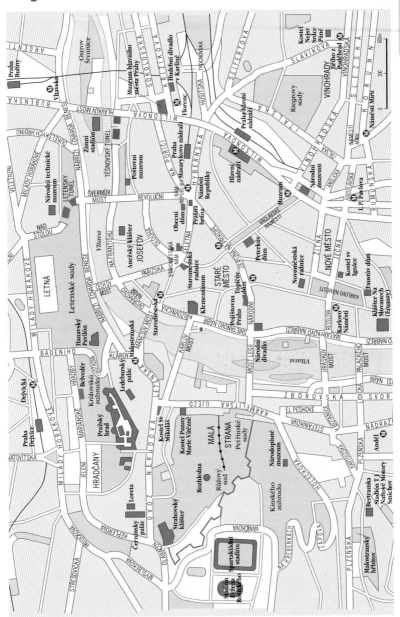

History

8th century AD
Libuše, a legendary princess, has a vision of a city on the river, to be built where a man is found constructing the threshold (*práh*) to his house. In a subsequent vision she sees a young ploughman (*přemysl*) who will marry her and found the Přemyslid line.

Late 9th century
Duke Bořivoj I, the first historically verified Přemyslid, founds a citadel (Hradčany) on the Vltava.

Tradition says 929, but more likely 935
Duke Wenceslas (later to become patron saint of Bohemia) is murdered by his brother Boleslav I.

1085
Vratislav II is made first King of Bohemia by Emperor Henry IV.

1257
Otakar II settles German merchants and artisans on the left bank of the Vltava river.

1306
The Přemyslid dynasty dies out.

1346
Prague's golden age begins with the accession of Charles IV of the Luxembourg dynasty. In 1355 he is crowned Holy Roman Emperor. Charles Bridge, St Vitus Cathedral, Karlštejn and the Týn Church are built.

1348
Nové Město and the Charles University (Karolinum) are founded.

1357
Construction of the Charles Bridge aids development on the east bank of the Vltava.

1415
Jan Hus, the religious reformer, is burned alive for heresy at the Council of Constance.

1419
First defenestration of Prague: Hussites throw councillors from the windows of the New Town Hall.

1458–71
The Hussite king George of Poděbrady rules in Bohemia.

1483 Second defenestration of Prague: the mayor is thrown from the windows of the Old Town Hall.

1526 Ferdinand I becomes the first Habsburg king of Bohemia. He brings the Jesuits to Prague in 1556.

1576–1611 Rudolf II invites scholars, artists and astronomers to his Prague court, among them Tycho Brahe and Johannes Kepler.

1618 Protestant nobles throw Ferdinand II's councillors from the windows of Prague

A window on history: Prague Castle, scene of the famous 1618 defenestration of Prague

Castle. This triggers the Thirty Years War.

1620 The Bohemian Protestants are defeated at the Battle of the White Mountain, and the Counter-Reformation is driven forward. Fine churches and palaces are built, but Prague is reduced to a backwater of the Habsburg Empire.

1740–80 Maria Theresa introduces enlightened reforms, but tries to expel the Jewish population from Prague.

1784 The four Prague towns of Hradčany, Malá Strana, Staré Město and Nové Město are amalgamated. Joseph II allows freedom of religion and abolishes serfdom, but enforces German as the language of state.

1790–1848 The rise of Czech national consciousness culminates in the unsuccessful revolution of 1848.

1918 At the end of World War I, the Republic of Czechoslovakia is founded. The architect of Czech independence, Tomáš Masaryk, is its first president.

1939 Prague's Jews are sent to concentration camps.

1948 The Communist Party seizes power.

1968 The 'Prague Spring', led by Alexander Dubček, is crushed by the Warsaw Pact invasion.

1989 The Communist regime collapses on 10 December. Václav Havel is elected president on 29 December.

Wenceslas I, Duke of Bohemia

Memorial to victims of Communism

1990	Following elections in June, a right-of-centre government is formed, and begins the transformation of Czechoslovakia into a market economy.
1993	On 1 January the Czech and Slovak Republics formally separate. Prague is the capital of the new Czech Republic.
1997	The Czechs prepare for their entry into the European Union and accept formal entry into NATO.
2004	On 1 May the Czech Republic joins the EU.
2007	The Czech Republic enters the Schengen Zone, border controls are scrapped.
2009	Prague considers a bid to host the 2020 Olympic Games after it failed to make the shortlist for 2016.

Politics

In the 19th century, Prague became the focus of the Czech national revival led by the distinguished historian František Palacký (1798–1876). Palacký refused to take part in the German National Assembly held in Frankfurt during the 1848 revolution against the reactionary Habsburg government, presiding over a Pan-Slav Congress in Prague instead: an unmistakeable signal that the days of German political and cultural domination were numbered.

The Republic

The man who realised Palacký's dream was Tomáš Garrigue Masaryk (1850–1937) (*see p102*). During World War I, Masaryk, in exile in the USA, persuaded the allies to recognise a new (Slavic) Czechoslovak state in the event of victory. On 28 October 1918 the Czechoslovak Republic was declared in Prague with Masaryk as president. The Slovaks soon grew restive under what they regarded as Czech hegemony, and the German-speaking border area of Sudetenland had to be occupied after attempting to break away. These developments had ominous implications for the future integrity of Czechoslovakia.

World War II and Communism

Hitler occupied the Sudetenland in 1938, and the rest of Bohemia and Moravia the following year. The latter remained directly under Nazi control during the war, but the Slovaks were allowed an 'autonomous' state. At the end of the war Edvard Beneš, the pre-war president, returned to his post and presided over the expulsion of most of the Sudeten Germans (nearly 2.5 million fled or were forced to leave).

The Communist Party quickly infiltrated the organs of government. It also enjoyed great popular support, not least because the 1938 betrayal of Czechoslovakia by Britain and France at Munich was still fresh in people's minds. In the 'Victorious February' of 1948, the Party consolidated its grip without taking up Stalin's offer of military assistance.

An unofficial sign proclaiming the new Czech Republic in 1993

The Prague Spring

After 15 years, pressure for reform began to grow, and the hardliners lost ground. In 1968, Slovak Alexander Dubček emerged as leader, and pledged to bring in 'socialism with a human face'. The Russians unleashed the Warsaw Pact invasion of August 1968, and Gustáv Husák reimposed orthodoxy, surviving (latterly as president) until the Velvet Revolution of 1989 (*see pp16–17*). Resistance to the invasion was non-violent and symbolic, most dramatically in the case of the student Jan Palach, who committed suicide on Wenceslas Square by setting fire to himself. Some 150,000 people fled the country during this critical period.

1989 and its consequences

A worsening economy, the more liberal regime of Mikhail Gorbachev in the USSR, and the opposition of Charter 77 (formed to monitor human rights) put increasing pressure on the regime, culminating in the 'Velvet Revolution' of November–December 1989, which swept Václav Havel to the presidency. The subsequent break-up of Czechoslovakia into two separate states on 1 January 1993 occurred without a public referendum; Prime Ministers Václav Klaus and Vladimír Mečiar did little to halt it on either side.

The Czech Republic (which consists of Bohemia and Moravia) is a pluralist democracy with a government elected by proportional representation. Václav Havel was elected president (by parliament) for a five-year term, although with powers considerably reduced from those that he himself believed he required.

The country has been subjected to a privatisation programme, and has enormous potential in areas such as tourism (currently focused on Prague) and foreign direct investment. Its problems are fairly similar to those of other former Soviet satellites.

Unemployment is around 6 per cent, though it is only 2 per cent in Prague. Currently, the Czech government is concentrating on judicial and legislative reform and improvements to the country's infrastructure. Today, Prague is an exciting place in which to live and work. Further developments are in the air, and the city glows with increasing affluence (unlike some regions where relatively high unemployment and slow development are still the norm).

Memorial to a modern-day hero: plaque commemorating student Jan Palach

The Velvet Revolution

After the crushing of the 'Prague Spring' in 1968, Czechoslovakia sank again under the oppression of Stalinism. Opposition began to surface with the formation of Charter 77. This monitored abuses of human rights in violation of the Helsinki Agreements to which the Communist government was a signatory.

By the mid-1980s, the Czechoslovak Stalinists found themselves increasingly undermined by Mikhail Gorbachev's policy of *perestroika*. Demands for more freedom came from young people, Charter 77 and the Catholic Church.

At the end of 1989 the organisations Civic Forum (in what was to become the Czech Republic) and People Against Violence (in Slovakia) were formed in response to police brutality during demonstrations that took place on 17 November.

The following week, vast crowds poured into Wenceslas Square every evening, demanding the resignation of the government. On Friday evening, Dubček addressed the crowds with Václav Havel, the leading personality of Civic Forum.

The Party tried forming a new government with puppet figures, but

President Václav Havel led the country to democratic stability

Peaceful 'Revolutionaries' left flowers and lit candles in Wenceslas Square

the tide was running against them. On 10 December the first cabinet since 1948 with Communists in a minority was announced, together with a promise of multi-party elections in June 1990. Posters immediately appeared with the slogan 'HAVEL NA HRAD!' (Havel to the Castle!), and demonstrations continued until he was elected president on 29 December.

The 'Velvet Revolution', as it was dubbed, was not pushing at an open door. Through massive peaceful demonstrations and the threat of a general strike, it defeated desperate and ruthless men. However, the deciding factor was the refusal of President Gorbachev to save the puppet regime maintained by his predecessors.

As soon as it was clear that the regime could not summon foreign tanks to save itself, it collapsed like a pack of cards.

Culture

'Prague always had two faces. She was officially German and unofficially Czech. Or she was officially Czech, but unofficially she had within herself a German city, with its own schools, universities, cinemas, theatres, restaurants, coffee-houses, newspapers. She was officially Austrian, and unofficially anti-Austrian. She was officially Catholic, and unofficially anti-Christian . . .'

WILLY LORENZ
To Bohemia with Love

The paradoxical nature of Prague and its people has constantly been reflected in the city's art, architecture and literature. Religious conflict has been

The strong architectural tradition in Prague continues with the Dancing House (1992–6)

linked to this from earliest times and has shaped the face of the city. Hussite mobs wrecked the interiors of churches, but the Jesuit-led Counter-Reformation, and later, towards the end of the 19th century, Art Nouveau, filled Prague with sensual, drama-filled architecture and images.

The pattern of victories and defeats the city has been through has produced a many-layered culture, part of it always submerged. Consequently, writer Paul Kornfeld described Prague as a 'metaphysical madhouse', and a place where 'the absurd is the paradoxical condition of human existence'.

In the 20th century, Czech artists and sculptors began to look to the West. Alphonse Mucha, the best-known Art Nouveau painter, and the abstract artist František Kupka lived in Paris, while the sculptor František Bílek studied there. Between the wars, the Devětsil (Nine Forces) movement produced Prague's own version of avant-garde art, architecture and literature.

Baroque St Nicholas Church in the Lesser Quarter (Malá Strana)

Culture

Art and architecture

Prague's rich heritage of architecture begins with the Romanesque buildings below street level, and three rotunda churches from the 11th and 12th centuries. Gothic architecture dominated the city from the mid-13th century (St Vitus Cathedral, Týn Church and St Agnes' Convent). Renaissance style, imported from Italy under the first Habsburgs, is represented above all by the Belvedere, or Summer Palace (1563), built by Ferdinand I. With the Counter-Reformation, Baroque style conquered all. Huge palaces and magnificent churches appeared in the 17th and 18th centuries (St Nicholas in Malá Strana, St Nicholas in Staré Město). This creative energy is clearly manifested in the works of such artists as Karel Škréta and Cosmas Asam. Sculpture was not far behind. Always liberally used to complement architecture, it reached a high point of expressiveness with Matthias Braun, Ferdinand Brokoff and others.

After a period of historicism, when architecture replicated earlier styles, Prague was swept by the sensuous lines of Art Nouveau at the end of the 19th century (see pp30–31), followed by pioneering experiments with Cubist architecture that are unique to the city (see pp46–7).

Images of Prague

Eloquent images of Prague have been captured by two great Czech photographers – Josef Sudek (1896–1976) and František Drtikol (1878–1961). Sudek is known for his brilliant series of shots (1924) documenting the final phase in seven centuries of building St Vitus Cathedral. Drtikol's cityscapes range from winter panoramas of ice-clad bridges to the covered stairways and secret alleys of the city.

Even more evocative are the haunting scenes painted by Jakob Schikaneder (1855–1924). *Nocturne in Prague* (1911) is typical: on a chill autumn evening a woman and child hurry into the shadows out of the glare of a gaslight. Schikaneder's is a world of eventide and

A guard outside Prague Castle, the largest ancient castle in the world

shadowy figures, of dark buildings splashed with light, and frozen cabmen waiting in snow-covered squares.

Powerful in a different way are the three expressionistic Prague landscapes by Oskar Kokoschka (1886–1980). The turbulent brushstrokes and the bold angle of vision are most striking in his version of *Charles Bridge and the Hradčany* (1935).

Ukrainian painter Alexandr Onishenko has captured Prague scenes since 1997 in what he terms 'New Impressionism'. He captures visions of the rooftops, trams and old buildings of Prague. His works, much in demand, are on sale at the **Jakubská Galerie** (*Jakubská 4, Praha 1; www.galeriejakubska.cz*).

Music

'Whoever is Czech is a musician' runs a proverb, and this was certainly the impression given in the Baroque and Romantic eras. Jan Stamic was the court composer in Mannheim; Antonín Rejcha (a great friend of Beethoven) is said to be one of the most underrated composers; the Italians celebrated Josef Mysliveček as '*il divino Boemo*'

Culture

The Marionette Theatre

The Mucha Museum, dedicated to the Czech artist Alphonse Mucha

(the divine Bohemian), while an appreciative audience in Prague gave Mozart his greatest success with the premiere of his opera *Don Giovanni* (*see p106*). The 19th century produced an outpouring of patriotic romantic music – including such works as *Má Vlast* (*My Country*) by Bedřich Smetana, the *Slavonic Dances* of Antonín Dvořák and the *Glagolitic Mass* of Leoš Janáček.

Literature and drama

At the start of the 20th century Prague produced a flowering of writing in German, most famously that of Franz Kafka (*see pp82–3*). Czech writing was chiefly known abroad for the realism of Karel Čapek and Jaroslav Hašek's comic masterpiece *The Good Soldier Švejk*; then came the contemporary wave of writers such as Václav Havel, Bohumil Hrabal, Ivan Klíma, Milan Kundera and Josef

CHANGES

After years of political changes, many Czech museums and galleries have now been restored and reopened. However, if you are planning to travel off the beaten track, it's worth double-checking the availability and opening hours of hotels, restaurants and cultural sites, as renovation work is still continuing.

Škvorecký, with works of surreal humour, eroticism and bleak irony.

The Nobel Prize-winning poet Jaroslav Seifert summed up the choice facing Czech writers in the 40 years of Communism: 'When an ordinary person stays silent, it may be a tactical manoeuvre. When a writer stays silent, he is lying.'

Today, the new wave of Czech writers includes young authors such as Michal Viewegh (*Bringing up Girls in Bohemia*), whose works are also available in other languages.

Delight in the detail: statue at Hlavní Nadraží station

Impressions

The approaches to Prague, usually through softly rolling hills followed by grey suburbs of panel-built flats, hardly prepare you for the prize at the journey's end. When you finally find yourself in the historic centre, it is as though a curtain has suddenly lifted, revealing a city within a city, jewels of architecture held in a time capsule. The French writer André Breton aptly described this city as 'the magic metropolis of old Europe'.

Despite its air of being suspended in time, Prague has undergone intensive renovation and reconstruction. After the Velvet Revolution of 1989,

dramatic changes occurred almost overnight. Long-term changes are still under way, but life is stabilising after the flux, uncertainty and drama of the early

Prague environs

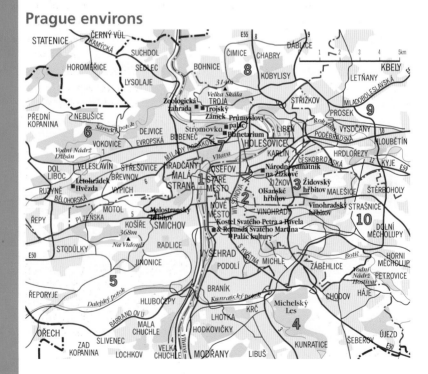

Impressions

1990s. Visitors may be surprised by the wealth of international brand names, stores such as Tesco and Julius Meinl, and the proliferation of international investors, law firms and businesses. Many old town houses have been renovated, and a wide range of shops, stores, hypermarkets and filling stations provide greater choices. Ultra-modern multi-screen cinema complexes are becoming increasingly commonplace. Decrepit, clattering Trabants and elderly Škodas are being replaced by standard 'Western' cars – indeed, Škoda itself now produces award-winning models such as the Fabia, Octavia, Superb and Roomster.

The backdrop to bustling city life is the cluster of diminutive, historic towns of old Prague. So rich in architectural beauty are these areas, it is little wonder that most Praguers are irrepressible local patriots. Rows of Baroque façades remind one of a film set (and are frequently used as such, as in *Mission: Impossible*, *Amadeus* and *The Lord of the Rings*, to name just a few), while palaces and churches cram the narrow streets of Malá Strana (the Lesser Quarter), and of Hradčany. Here, and in Staré Město (the Old Town), many of these are ancient cobbled alleyways from which cars have long been banned.

In these backwaters, Prague's uniquely ambivalent atmosphere of magic and menace can most powerfully be sensed. An exotic cast of emperors, warlords, religious fanatics, mystical rabbis and people of many different races have left their mark on the ancient core of the city. The past is a babble of competing voices, the present a vibrant metropolis. Prague remains, as Egon Erwin Kisch described it, 'the marketplace of sensations'.

When to go

Prague can be uncomfortably hot in high summer and very cold and raw in winter. The best time to visit the city (and Central Europe generally) is late spring or early autumn. It is not warm before April, and gets rapidly colder after October.

Many Praguers traditionally leave town in summer and head for their *chaty* (chalets) or *chalupy* (cottages) in the country. They now have an added incentive to do so, for the city is full of tourists, particularly in July and August. Although new facilities are being built and old ones expanded, it is still preferable to avoid these two months, as well as Whitsun and Easter. Also keep in mind that a number of sights

The narrow streets of the Old Town (Staré Město) are full of hidden delights

(especially castles and palaces and their gardens) may be closed in winter.

Getting around

From the visitor's point of view both the topography of Prague and its public transport system are decidedly user-friendly. The main sights are in the compact historic areas of the city (*see pp6–8*) and are ideally visited on foot. The heart of Staré Město is a pedestrian zone, as is most of Wenceslas Square and the whole of the castle area.

Buses

Buses serve outlying areas. You are only likely to use them for excursions and a few specific city destinations.

Car

Since the old city is compact and public transport runs up to the edge of its pedestrian zones, there is little point in driving around Prague. Moreover, the local driving style is aggressive and erratic, street parking is problematic, and being clamped or towed away is the common fate of unwary tourists. It is best to leave your car in a secure garage (*see p181*).

Metro

Three lines crisscross the city. If you take a private room in the suburbs, check that it is close to the metro. Trains run every 4 to 10 minutes at rush hours, every 6 minutes off-peak. A single ticket entitles you to ride the entire system for 75 minutes.

Trams are an attractive alternative to the metro

Remember that *výstup* means exit and *přestup* indicates an interchange, and you should have few problems.

Taxis

Taxis are plentiful, and relatively cheap by Western standards. Since the drivers know this, overcharging is common; it is always advisable to check that the meter is turned on (*zapněte taxametr, prosím* is the Czech for requesting this). If you are overcharged, ask for a receipt (*prosím dejte mi potrzení*) and write down the cabbie's number. Avoid picking up taxis from the airport and the Old Town Square as these are ruthlessly expensive. It is cheaper to dial **AAA** (*Tel: 14014 or 222 333 222*) and ask to be picked up from wherever you are.

Tram

The best way to see the city is by tram. Trams run along both banks of the Vltava, and cross the bridges to traverse Malá Strana as far as the northern approach to the castle. For sightseeing, the No 22 tram is the best, running from the New Town to the castle.

Pollution in Prague

'Forests dead or dying, rivers dirtied, air unbreathable, soil choked with chemicals.' That is how one publication described the environmental disaster facing the former Czechoslovakia. In addition to acid rain, water pollution and rivers incapable of supporting fish life, the country's air pollution, as measured by sulphur dioxide emissions per sq km, was the worst in Europe after that of (former) East Germany. The problem in Prague itself is worst in winter because of 'inversion', which traps cold air in the Prague basin, preventing sulphur dioxide from factories, and nitrogen oxide from motor vehicles, from escaping.

The government has attempted to improve the situation within the constraints of sparse budgets. Brown coal has been replaced as an energy source, wherever possible, to significant effect. This means retaining the nuclear power plant at Temelín, which is now fully functional despite years of delays. Neighbouring countries, in particular Austria, and a group of Czechs, fearing another Chernobyl, are lobbying for its closure.

Less controversial is the law requiring all cars sold on the Czech market to have a catalytic converter. Recycling programmes are very popular, with separate containers for white and coloured glass, paper and plastic bottles. Monitoring of air pollution is standard in the media. All this has made some headway, but the massive investment required for the decommissioning or modernisation of polluting factories, and the cleaning-up of water supplies, will still take years to materialise.

Manners and mores

Czechs attach great importance to courtesy: failure to greet your neighbours in the lift or on the stairs, if you are living in a private apartment, could well be taken amiss. Similarly, if you share a café or restaurant table (and you may find you have to), a *dobrý den* (good day) when you sit down and *a na shledanou* (goodbye) when you leave are *de rigueur*. Friendliness in restaurants and shops is more common than it was, and customer service is improving.

Central European housewives are extremely houseproud. Offer to remove your shoes on arrival at a flat. Women have always played a very active role in society, although as elsewhere they continue to juggle full-time jobs with the burden of domestic responsibilities.

The cost of living

The arrival of democracy and free-market policies exacted a high toll in terms of unemployment and spiralling prices. Still, Prague will seem reasonable to most visitors: rooms in private houses, meals and such items as concert tickets may cost as little as half of Western European prices.

Impressions

Prague

'The extraordinary historical treasures of Prague make the city worth the closest observation. It would be a foolish enterprise to write a history of the world without previously visiting this ancient capital.'

CHARLES SEALSFIELD,
German writer (1793–1864)

Anežský klášter (St Agnes' Convent)

The Convent of St Agnes is a particularly fine example of painstakingly restored early Gothic architecture. It was founded at the instigation of Agnes, the sister of Wenceslas I, in 1234; she preferred the relative freedom of life in a convent to the less attractive proposition of a dynastic marriage.

In 1235 Agnes became the first abbess of the new foundation, which was occupied by the mendicant order of Poor Clares. Some five years later, the Franciscans, male counterparts of the Poor Clares, settled in a monastery next door. The whole complex was sometimes referred to as the 'Bohemian Assisi', after the Italian town where, only a few years earlier, the two orders were founded side by side. There was also a Minorite monastery nearby, remains of which were discovered in the course of 20th-century restoration.

History

Both Agnes and Wenceslas are buried here, as are other members of the Přemyslid dynasty. Notwithstanding the convent's significance as a dynastic burial place (or perhaps because of it), it was vandalised during the Hussite wars (*see p39*) and the inmates compelled to leave. It was not until 1556 that it was reoccupied – by the Dominicans. The Poor Clares returned in 1627 and remained until 1782.

Emperor Joseph II dissolved the convent in 1782 on the grounds that it served no useful purpose. It was turned into an old people's home and, in the succeeding hundred years, fell into decay. Some parts became a slum, while others were a rabbit warren of craftsmen's studios. In the 1890s, a patriotic fund was inaugurated to clean up the area and restore the buildings.

It was in 1989, on the eve of the Velvet Revolution, shortly before Pope John Paul II's historic visit to Prague, that the first abbess of the Order of the Poor Clares was canonised.

The buildings

The cloister, dating to about 1260, is an open arcade around a square courtyard. It has a heavy vaulted ceiling characteristic of early Gothic. To the east, reached through a passage, is the most impressive of the surviving buildings, the **Kostel svatého Salvátora** (**Church of the Holy Saviour**). An interesting feature of this French-influenced Gothic church is the relief portraits on the capitals of the arched entrance, apparently those of the kings and queens of the Přemyslid dynasty. The head over the salvation altar is thought by scholars to be that of St Agnes herself, watching over the nearby entrance to the royal crypt.

One of the loveliest areas of the church is that of the choir.

South of the Church of the Holy Saviour is the **Kostel svatého Františka** (**Church of St Francis**), dating to about 1240, a somewhat severe edifice built according to the puritanical architectural norms laid down by the Minorites. King Wenceslas I is buried in this church, which has only recently reacquired a roof. It is now used for lectures and frequent concerts.

The convent also houses the Czech National Gallery's collections of art and sculpture (*see p110*) and a range of temporary exhibitions.
Anežská 1. Josefov, Praha I.
Tel: 224 810 628. Open: Tue–Sun 10am–6pm. Admission charge.
Trams: 5, 8 & 14 to Revolucní.

The interior of St Agnes' Convent

Art Nouveau architecture

Art Nouveau, a term first used in Paris in 1895, liberated architecture and the fine arts from rigid formalism and quotation. The natural world was its touchstone; it luxuriated in decorative flowing lines with floral patterns and exotic ornament.

When Art Nouveau arrived in Prague, much of Central European architecture seemed frozen in time. Those who gave the big commissions – principally the State and the Church – expected architects to adhere to the styles of the past. After a while, this so-called 'historicism' began to degenerate into a sterile and pompous reproduction of motifs from pattern books. Art Nouveau not only represented a new aesthetic approach, but also took advantage of advances in construction technology, using materials such as cast iron, steel and glass.

Prague contains some of the most fascinating Art Nouveau works in the world, though here they are usually labelled 'modern style' or *secesní* after the Viennese Secession movement. One of the most successful proponents of the new style in Paris was the Czech Alphonse Mucha (1860–1939), renowned for his enduringly popular posters. You can see some of his work in the Mayor's Hall, which is the highlight of a visit to the beautifully renovated Obecní dům (the Municipal House on Náměstí Republiky, *see pp124–5*), completed in 1911 and, perhaps, the most ambitious and visually stunning of Prague's Secessionist buildings.

Evropa hotel (Europa Hotel)

This sadly shabby but highly ornate hotel (*see p174*) is essential viewing for anyone nostalgic about a world that died in 1914. It was built in 1903–5 by Alois Dryák and Bedřich Bendelamayer. *25 Václavské náměstí. Tel: 224 228 215. www.evropahotel.cz. Café open: 7am–11pm. Metro: Muzeum or Můstek.*

Art Nouveau window in St Vitus Cathedral

Hanavský pavilón (Hanava Pavilion)

Built for the Paris World Exhibition of 1878, the pavilion is a beautiful folly. The use of cast iron in the construction gives it an Art Nouveau flavour. There is an expensive but good restaurant here. *Letenské sady. Tel: 233 323 641. Open: daily 11am–1am. Terrace café open: summer, sunrise–sunset. Trams: 12 & 17 to Čechův Most, then climb the steps up to the park.*

Josef Fanta's Central Station

Hlavní nádraží (Central Railway Station)

One of the most monumental of Prague's Art Nouveau buildings, the façade and concourse for the station were designed by Josef Fanta in 1909. The building is undergoing complete renovation, due for completion in 2010. *Wilsonova. Metro: (line C) Hlavní nádraží.*

Peterkův dům (Peterka House)

A rather restrained example of Art Nouveau by Jan Kotěra, a pupil of the great Viennese Secessionist architect Otto Wagner. *12 Václavské náměstí. Not open to the public. Metro: Muzeum or Můstek.*

Pojišťovna Praha (Prague Savings Bank) and Topičův dům (Topič Publishing House)

The buildings, Nos 7 and 9 respectively, are neighbours on Národní. Note the lavish mosaic lettering above the windows, advertising the bank's various services, and the ceramic reliefs in the gable of the Topič Publishing House. Both houses were designed by Oswald Polívka and built between 1907 and 1908 (*see pp44–5*). *7 & 9 Národní. Not open to the public. Trams: 6, 9, 18, 21, 22 & 23 to Národní divadlo.*

Průmyslový palác (Industrial Palace)

Bedřich Münzberger's huge steel and glass construction, built for the Bohemia Jubilee Exhibition of 1891, is the first Prague building that recognisably embodies the spirit of Art Nouveau. It still has neo-Baroque features, but the materials used were innovative. *Praha 7, Výstaviště. Open: May–Sept 10am–5.30pm. Free admission except evenings. Metro: Nádraží Holešovice. Trams: 5, 12, 14, 15 & 17 to Výstaviště.*

Those hungry for more can pick up an interesting, beautifully illustrated booklet entitled *Art Nouveau in Prague* by Petr Balajka, available at many bookshops.

The Vltava

The Vltava (Moldau to the Germans) dominates Prague as few other rivers dominate a capital city. In the past, whole sections of the population used to live off it, though it had less appealing roles as well: thieves and adulterers were suspended in its icy waters in wicker baskets from the Charles Bridge; John Nepomuk, the 14th-century canon who supported his archbishop against King Wenceslas IV, was thrown into it and drowned.

The once wild river is now tamed by six dams along its 430km (267 mile) course. But in August 2002, several days of continuous heavy rain caused the Vltava to burst its banks. The effects were devastating: along its length, 200,000 people had to be evacuated from their homes, and

A statue of the water nymph Terezka, the female spirit of the Vltava

The Vltava offers great views of the city

watermarks can still be seen on houses next to the river in Prague.

Unfortunately, the river remains unhealthy. Vltava fish featured on Prague menus have to be caught upstream from where the dangerously polluted Berounka flows into the main river – a sad decline from the Middle Ages, when the city's apprentices complained that they were fed salmon every day.

The romantic image of the river is preserved in the city's memorials to it. For instance, the Vltava water nymph (known affectionately as 'Terezka') may be seen on the wall of the Clam-Gallas Palace's gardens on Mariánské náměstí. The most beloved monument is on the northern tip of the Dětský ostrov (the Children's Island). From here, wreaths for the river's many victims are thrown into the water in November. On All Souls' Day, a boat decked with black flags sets out on the dark waters as the city commemorates its dead.

Belvedér

It was between 1538 and 1563 that the Královská zahrada (Royal Gardens, *see p48 & p51*) and a surpassingly elegant *Lustschloss* (summer residence) took shape on a patch of land a little to the northeast of Hradčany. This was the summer palace built by Ferdinand I for his wife, Anna Jagiello; the design and its garden setting show a strong Italian influence.

The original architect of the Belvedere (as the palace is known), Paolo della Stella, was responsible for the slim-columned arcade with its mythological reliefs that gives the palace its southern look, and reminds one that it was a retreat for the court in the warm months. Bonifaz Wohlmut, the court architect who also built the Ball Game Court in the gardens, completed the ambitious project between 1552 and 1569. His design of the copper roof is unusual, like the hull of an upturned ship, which has now turned a mellow green through oxidisation.

Rudolf II, Ferdinand's grandson, was particularly fond of the Belvedere, and encouraged his Danish astronomer, Tycho Brahe, to set up an observatory on the terrace. After Brahe's death, Johannes Kepler, who had been Brahe's assistant and went on to become a brilliant astronomer in his own right, succeeded him as imperial mathematician. Kepler's *Laws of Planetary Motion,* published in 1609, were based on work done at the Belvedere.

Spectacular ceiling frescoes in the Břevnov Monastery

The Swedes plundered the palace in 1648, and Joseph II turned it into a military laboratory. A proper restoration was undertaken only in the mid-19th century, when a cycle of historical paintings dealing with the leitmotifs of Bohemian history was added to the first-floor rooms. *Hradčany, Praha 1. Open: during exhibitions only. Admission charge. Trams: 18 & 20 to Chotkovy Sady.*

Bývalý benediktinský klášter (Břevnov Monastery)

Legend has it that Duke Boleslav II and Bishop Adalbert of Prague were joint founders of Břevnov Monastery in 993, which would make it the oldest monastery in Bohemia. The site of the monastery was supposedly revealed to them in a dream. Such cooperation would be remarkable, if true, in that it predates the massacre of Adalbert's (Slavník) family by their rivals for power, Boleslav's (Přemyslid) family, by only two years.

Apart from the crypt, there are hardly any Romanesque or Gothic architectural remains. The church, once dedicated to St Adalbert, was probably rededicated to St Margaret in the second half of the 14th century after her remains were transferred here in the 13th century. What we see today is the result of a complete rebuilding in Baroque style, between 1708 and 1745, by Christoph Dientzenhofer.

Dientzenhofer and his son, Kilián Ignác, turned Břevnov into one of the glories of Bohemian Baroque. The Kostel svaté Markéty (St Margaret's Church) is a masterwork of visionary architecture. Its marching series of diagonally protruding pillars supports oval ceiling spaces covered with frescoes. The tightly focused effect recalls Dientzenhofer's Church of St Nicholas in Malá Strana.

Other highlights include the frescoes in the Prelates' Hall by Cosmas Asam. The Library also has fine allegorical frescoes by Felix Scheffler, and the Refectory is notable for Bernhard Spinetti's stucco and Jan Kovář's manneristic painting on the ceiling.

The monastery has undergone complete restoration in recent years. The Communists had turned it into an archive, but the Benedictines are now back at Břevnov.

Markétská 1, Praha 6. Open for tours: Apr–Oct Sat & Sun 10am, 2pm, 4pm; Nov–Mar Sat & Sun 10am & 2pm. Trams: 15, 22 & 25, alighting at Břevnovský klášter.

The Belvedere Summer Palace, built by Ferdinand I, the first Habsburg king of Bohemia

CEMETERIES

Malostranský hřbitov (Lesser Quarter Cemetery)

Opened in 1680 for plague victims, the graveyard continued in use until 1884. *Praha 5. Trams: 4, 7, 9 & 10 to Plzeňská ulice, Bertramka.*

Olšanské hřbitov (Olšany Cemetery)

One of the biggest cemeteries of Central Europe, with over 100,000 graves. *Praha 3, Vinohradská třída.* *Trams: 5, 10, 11, 16 & 26. Metro: Flora.*

Starý židovský hřbitov (Old Jewish Cemetery)

See pp78–9.

Vinohradský hřbitov (Vinohrady Cemetery)

Celebrated artists, actors, singers and writers are buried here. *Praha 10, Vinohradská třída.* *Trams: 11 & 26.*

Vyšehradský hřbitov (Vyšehrad Cemetery)

Celebrities buried here include the composers Antonín Dvořák and Bedřich Smetana. *Praha 2, Vyšehrad. Metro: Vyšehrad.*

Židovský hřbitov (Jewish Cemetery)

Franz Kafka's grave is in section 21, row 14, at No 33. *Trams: 11, 16, 19 & 26.* *Metro: Želivského/Flora.*

Central Prague

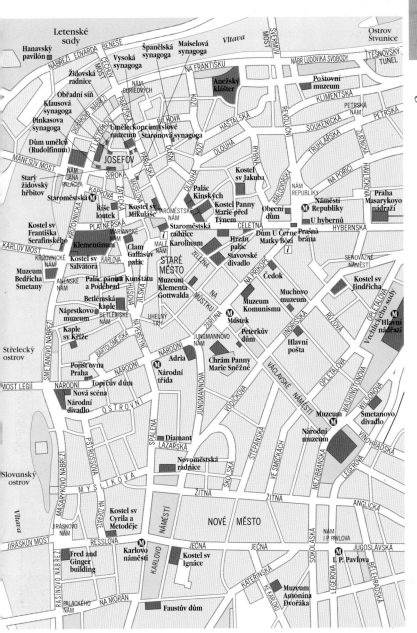

Churches

Prague boasts an astonishing wealth of ecclesiastical architecture. By the end of the 14th century there were 26 convents and monasteries in the city; scores of churches were built in the Middle Ages, the Baroque period and the 19th century. This list of churches includes ones not covered under Hradčany, Staroměstské náměstí and Malostranské náměstí. It excludes churches attached to convents where the latter have their own entries. Where access is limited, this has been noted.

Betlémská kaple (Bethlehem Chapel)

The present building is a modern replica of the Gothic trapezoidal chapel founded in 1391. It was rebuilt between 1536 and 1539, acquired by the Jesuits in 1661 and virtually demolished in 1786.

The 14th-century Church authorities, who had agreed to the construction of a 'chapel', were faced with a building that could accommodate 3,000, was a focus of church reform and would become a lasting spiritual centre of Hussitism – Jan Hus himself preached at the chapel.

In the adjoining preacher's house are exhibits relating to the Hussites, and a reconstruction of a 15th-century domestic interior.

Staré Město. Betlémské náměstí.
Open: Apr–Oct Tue–Sun 10am–6.30pm, Nov–Mar Tue–Sun 10am–5.30pm.
Admission charge.
Metro: Můstek or Národní třída.

Chrám Panny Marie Sněžné (Church of Our Lady of the Snows)

This building was planned as a coronation cathedral by Charles IV, but construction had got no further than the lofty choir before being interrupted by

Jan Hus presides over Old Town Square

JAN HUS (c.1373–1415)

Born of peasant stock in southern Bohemia, Hus had a meteoric career in the Church, ending up confessor to the Queen, and Rector of Charles University. He was influenced by the English religious reformer John Wycliffe (c.1320–84) and became the greatest preacher of his day. He collided with the Church on the issue of selling indulgences to finance papal wars, and was summoned to the Council of Constance in 1415 where, despite the Emperor Sigismund's personal guarantee of safe conduct, he was convicted of heresy and burned at the stake.

In Prague there erupted riots directed against the Church and its corrupt clerics. The Hussite wars that followed (1419–34) ended with an agreement at Basel between the Catholic Church and the more moderate wing of the Hussites. It was only in 1965 that the Vatican overturned Hus's conviction for heresy.

The Bethlehem Chapel is a modern replica of an earlier building

the Hussite rebellion. Jan Želivský, the radical reformer, was buried here after his execution in 1421. The angry demonstration that ended with the first defenestration of Prague began in Our Lady of the Snows on 30 July 1419. *Nové Město, Jungmannovo náměstí. Metro station: Můstek.*

Kostel svatého Cyrila a Metoděje (Church of St Cyril and St Methodius)

This somewhat forbidding church, completed by Kilián Dientzenhofer in 1740, was originally dedicated to St Charles Borromeo. When the Czech Orthodox Church took it over as their cathedral in 1935, it was rededicated to St Cyril and St Methodius. The crypt contains memorials to resistance fighters who took refuge there after assassinating the Nazi governor of Bohemia in 1942. *Nové Město, Resslova ulice. Admission at times other than for Mass is difficult. Metro: Karlovo náměstí. Crypt open: Nov–Feb Tue–Sun 10am–4pm, Mar–Oct Tue–Sun 10am–5pm. Admission charge.*

Kostel svatého Františka Serafinského (Church of St Francis Seraphicus)

This richly decorated church (1689) is notable for its imposing cupola with V L Reiner's fresco of *The Last Judgement* (1722) and for its walls clad in Bohemian marble. *Staré Město, Křížovnické náměstí. Trams: 17 & 18 to Karlovy Lázně. Metro: Staroměstská.*

Kostel svatého Jakuba
(Church of St James)

St James's is a Baroque reconstruction of an earlier Gothic building (*see p131*). The long, glittering interior is furnished with 21 elegantly carved altars, above which are open galleries and a magnificent series of frescoes (*The Life of the Virgin* and *The Adoration of the Trinity* by Franz Guido Voget). The altarpiece is Václav Reiner's version of *The Martyrdom of St James*. The impressive marble and sandstone tomb in the left-hand nave is of Count Vratislav of Mitrovic, a Bohemian Chancellor.

Staré Město, Malá Štupartská.
Metro: Náměstí Republiky or Můstek.

The Church of St James in the Old Town, one of the loveliest churches in Prague

Kostel svatého Jana
Nepomuckého na Skalce
(Church of St John Nepomuk
on the Rock)

This is one of the architect Kilián Ignác Dientzenhofer's masterworks. A double flight of balustraded steps sweeps up to the twin-towered late-Baroque façade (1739). Inside, the ceiling fresco of *The Ascension of St John Nepomuk* by Karel Kovář is of exceptional quality, as is Jan Brokoff's altar statue of the saint, a model for the version later placed on Charles Bridge.

Nové Město, Vyšehradská třída.
Admission at times other than for Mass is difficult. Trams: 3, 4, 10, 14, 16, 18 & 24 to Karlovo náměstí.
Metro: Karlovo náměstí.

Kostel Nanebevzetí Panny Marie
a Karla Velikého
(Church of the Assumption of Our
Lady and Charlemagne)

Charles IV founded the monastery (part of the former Augustinian monastery known as Karlov) in 1350, and stipulated that the design for the church should follow that of Charlemagne's Imperial Chapel at Aachen, but some of the building's finest parts (such as the remarkable star vaulting) were completed by Bonifaz Wohlmut only in the 16th century. The pilgrims' steps on the south side are a Baroque addition, modelled on the Scala Santa in Rome. Don't miss the side galleries with theatrical sculptures by J J Schlansovsk (*The Annunciation* and *Christ Before Pilate*).

Nové Město, Ke Karlovu.
Metro: I P Pavlova.

Kostel Nejsvětějšího Srdce Páně (Church of the Sacred Heart)

Anyone with an interest in architecture should visit this, a stunning example of Josip Plečnik's work, built in 1933 under the influence of the Viennese school of Otto Wagner. At the east end is a massive pedimental tower with a gigantic clock set in it like a rose window – a foretaste of contemporary postmodernism. The interior, though functionalist, has nobility and grace. Look for the stylised wooden statues of Bohemian saints by Damian Pesan, who also sculpted the monumental gilded Christ.

Praha 3, Náměstí Jiřího z Poděbrad.
Metro: Jiřího z Poděbrad.

Kostel Panny Marie Vítězné (Church of St Mary the Victorious)

This was Prague's first Baroque church (1613), ironically commissioned by Lutherans – since the Baroque style is associated with militant Catholicism. The Carmelites later rebuilt it. Inside is the *Bambino di Praga*, a Spanish wax model of the infant Jesus, with supposed miraculous powers. It is an object of great Catholic veneration, and wears a spectacular array of clothing which is changed according to religious festivals.

Malá Strana, Karmelitská ulice.
Trams: 12, 20, 22 & 23 to Hellichova.

Kostel svatého Tomáše (Church of St Thomas)

Kilián Ignác Dientzenhofer remodelled this church in Baroque style in 1731.

Traces can be seen of earlier rebuildings of the Romanesque original in Gothic and Renaissance style. Ceiling frescoes by Václav Reiner depict the *Life of St Augustine* (in the cupola) and the *Legend of St Thomas*. Karel Škréta, one of the greatest of Prague's early Baroque painters, did several of the altarpieces. Over the high altar are copies of *The Martyrdom of St Thomas* and *St Augustine*, commissioned for the church from Flemish painter Peter Paul Rubens (1577–1640). The originals are in the National Gallery.

Buried in the cloister is an English humanist poetess at the court of Rudolf II, Elizabeth Jane Weston (or 'Vestonia' under her Latin *nom de plume*).

Mála Strana, Letenská ulice.
Trams: 12, 20, 22 & 23 to Malostranské náměstí. Metro: Malostranská.

The Church of the Sacred Heart in Vinohrady is a Modernist masterpiece

Walk: Churches of Nové Město

This walk gives a taste of the rich heritage left by Prague's two great waves of Gothic and Baroque church building in the Nové Město (New Town).

Allow 2 hours.

Begin at Karlovo náměstí metro station (line B), take Karlovo náměstí exit, and walk downhill along Resslova.

1 Kostel svatého Cyrila a Metoděje (Church of St Cyril and St Methodius)

On your right is the Church of St Cyril and St Methodius, the Czech Orthodox cathedral (*see p39*). A plaque on the wall reminds you that it was here that

the Free Czech agents who assassinated the Nazi governor of Bohemia, Reinhard Heydrich, made their last stand on 18 June 1942 (*see p98 & p142*). Across the street is **Kostel svatého Václava (St Wenceslas Church)**. The Hussite congregation, which now owns

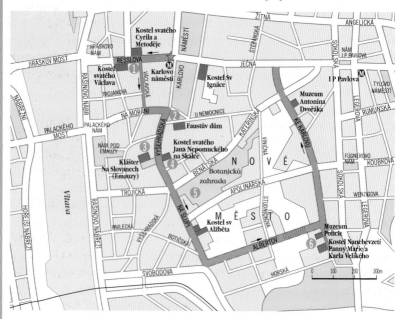

St Wenceslas, is the successor to the warring Hussites suppressed by the Counter-Reformation.

Walk back up Resslova, turn right into Václavská, and go as far as Na Moráni. Turn left up to the junction with Vyšehradská, then right.

2 Faustův dům (Faust House)

On the corner with U nemocnice is the Baroque Faustův dům where the opening scene of the Czech version of the Faust legend takes place. Rudolf II's alchemist, Edward Kelley, is supposed to have lived in an earlier house here.

Walk straight on.

3 Klášter Na Slovanech (Emmaus Monastery)

One of the few buildings in Prague to suffer bomb damage in the war. The most dramatic aspects of its restoration are the two reinforced concrete sail-like spires.

Continue further along on the left.

4 Kostel svatého Jana Nepomuckého na Skalce (Church of St John Nepomuk on the Rock)

This church (*see p40*) is one of Kilián Dientzenhofer's loveliest Baroque creations. It is difficult to access (although you may be able to do so during Mass), but even from the outside you can admire how the architect has cunningly turned to advantage the steep and narrow site on which this elegant little church is perched.

Floral delights in the Botanická zahrada

As Vyšehradská merges into Na slupi, you can turn off left into the Botanical Garden.

5 Botanická zahrada (Botanical Garden)

The glasshouse of exotic flora is worth the small entrance charge, and you can lose yourself happily for half an hour among the dense shrubbery and meandering paths (*see p48*).

Continue along Na slupi and turn left up Albertov. Climb the steps at the end on to Ke Karlovu.

6 Kostel Nanebevzetí Panny Marie a Karla Velikého (Church of the Assumption of Our Lady and Charlemagne)

See p40.

The Muzeum Policie (Police Museum) is adjacent to the church. You return along Ke Karlovu, passing the Muzeum Antonína Dvořáka (Antonín Dvořák Museum – Vila Amerika; *see pp106–7*) on the way.

Trams to the centre leave from Ječná.

Walk: Churches of Nové Město

Walk: Nové Město

'New' is a decidedly relative term in Prague: the original Nové Město was founded by Charles IV as long ago as 1348. The king created this new quarter of the city to link Staré Město with the fortress of Vyšehrad. In the late 19th century the area was largely reconstituted, and a slum was transformed into streets and squares exuding middle-class respectability and self-confidence.

Allow 1 hour.

Begin at Národní divadlo (trams 6, 9, 18, 21, 22 & 23) and walk east along Národní.

1 Along Národní třída

On your right is Kostel svaté Voršily (the Ursuline Church), which is occasionally open so that its Baroque frescoes can be admired. Outside is a striking statue of St John Nepomuk; according to the legend, he was thrown into the Vltava on 20 March 1393, on the orders of Wenceslas IV, for refusing to reveal the secrets of the Queen's confession.

Across the street are two exceptionally fine examples of Art Nouveau architecture, the Pojišťovna Praha (Prague Savings Bank) at No 7 and the Topičův dům (Topič Publishing House) at No 9.

Further up the street on the right (No 16), a small shrine under an arcade commemorates the victims of police brutality on 17 November 1989 that triggered the 'Velvet Revolution'.

2 Jungmannovo náměstí (Jungmann Square)

At the end of Národní is Jungmannovo náměstí, named after Josef Jungmann, a leading figure of the 19th-century Czech literary revival, whose statue dominates the square. To the south is the Cubist Adria Palace, with a pleasant terrace café. The basement contains a theatre where Civic Forum used to meet after 17 November 1989.

On the eastern edge of the square is the celebrated Cubist lamppost, which stands close to the entrance to Chrám Panny Marie Sněžné (Church of Our Lady of the Snows, *see pp38–9*). Charles IV planned this as a great coronation church, but the money ran out when only the chancel had been completed.

Turn left out of the church.

3 Františkánská zahrada (Franciscan Gardens)

You soon come to the entrance to the Františkánská zahrada to the southeast, part of the Franciscan monastery that ranges along their northwest wall. The gardens are a pleasant place to eat a picnic lunch picked up from one of the many shops on Václavské náměstí (Wenceslas Square).

Returning to Jungmannovo náměstí, bear left down Jungmannova. Just beyond the junction with Vodičkova, Karlovo náměstí begins. On the way you can detour to U Fleků, where a famous black beer is brewed on the premises (see pp170–71). Turn right into Lazarská, go through a passageway at Spálená 15 into Opatovická, then turn left for Křemencova 11. The beer hall is on your right. Retrace your steps to the end of Lazarská, then turn right into Vodičkova.

4 Novoměstská radnice (New Town Hall)

On your right is the ancient-looking Novoměstská radnice. The tower, entrance hall and cellars are genuinely medieval. The first defenestration of Prague took place here in 1419 when Hussites threw Catholic councillors out of the windows for refusing to release reformist prisoners.

Trams back to the centre may be picked up on Ječná, which traverses Karlovo náměstí.

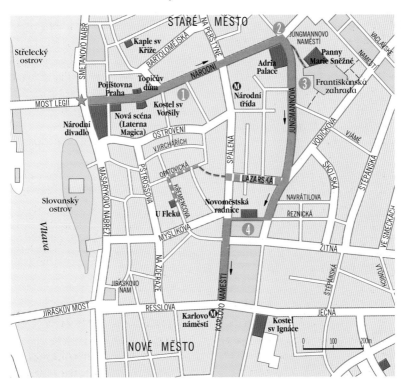

Cubist architecture

In 1910 the appropriately named Czech painter Bohumil Kubišta wrote excitedly home from Paris informing his colleagues that Picasso and Braque were the artists of the future. There followed a vogue in Prague for Cubist painting and Cubist design in the applied arts and architecture. In 1911 the influential Skupina výtvarných umělců (Group of Fine Artists) was established, with its own journal, and overnight (or so it seemed) Cubist houses appeared, filled with Cubist furniture and Cubist household articles.

A Cubist streetlamp

The rapid acceptance of Cubism (and Modernism generally) demonstrated the Czech determination to overcome their historical status as a provincial backwater. Cubism was attractive to artists and intellectuals who thought of Czech culture as part of the European mainstream; yet it was natural that there should be something characteristically 'Czech' about the local variants of Modernism. Cubist buildings by Josef Gočár (1880–1948), Josef Chochol (1880–1956) and Pavel Janák (1882–1956) recall Bohemian Baroque in their harmonious proportions and geometrical play of surfaces. Indeed, one of the earliest Cubist buildings by Gočár was accepted by the general public because it harmonised with its Baroque neighbours on Celetná ulice.

After the founding of the Czechoslovak Republic, Cubism developed into a 'National Style' or 'Rondocubism', intended as an expression of 'Slav' identity, but with both Cubist and traditional features. The façade of Janák's Rondocubist Adria Palace, which mixes all three elements, brings to mind a futuristic Italian Renaissance palace.

Although abstract form is central in Cubism, the play of geometrical surfaces in Prague's Cubist buildings

BUILDINGS

Josef Chochol: Neklanova ulice 30 and
Libušina ulice 3. Trams: 7, 18 & 24 to Na
slupi. Rašínovo nábřeží 6–10.
Trams: 3, 7, 16, 17 & 21 to Výtoň.
Josef Gočár: Dům U Černé Matky Boží
(Black Madonna House), Celetná ulice 19.
Metro: Náměstí Republiky. Bank Legií, Na
poříčí 24. Metro: Náměstí Republiky.
Pavel Janák: Adria Palace, Jungmannova 31.
Metro: Národní třída or Můstek.
Emil Králíček: Diamond House, Spálená
ulice 4. Metro: Národní třída.
Otakar Novotný: Ulice Elišky
Krásnohorské 123. Tram: 17 to Pravnická
fakulta.

provides a sensuality far removed
from the arid anonymity of much
modern architecture. Some people are
impressed by their boldness, others
find them sinister; either way, these
buildings are impossible to ignore.

In 1912 Josef Gočár built the Dům
u Černé Matky Boží (Black Madonna
House) on Celetná ulice. It was so-
called because a Baroque statue of
the Madonna from the previous

Janák's Rondocubist Adria Palace

house on the site was retained on the
façade. There are four storeys, the
first three of which consist almost
entirely of windows, so that the
building seems to be all eyes and no
face. Josef Chochol built more Cubist
houses than any of his colleagues,
whose designs often remained on
paper. On Neklanova ulice in
Vyšehrad is perhaps his most famous
building, an apartment block with
wedge-shaped forms on the façade
and an overhanging cornice. Chochol
designed the nearby Kovařovičova Vila
on Libušina ulice, where even the
garden and railings are Cubist. On
Rašínovo nábřeží is his three-family
house (Rodinný trojdům), described as
being 'like a classical palace', perhaps
because of its relief-covered
pediment.

On Ulice Elišky Krásnohorské is
Otakar Novotný's Rondocubist
building, one of the first to have a
façade enlivened by colour contrasts.
The best-known Rondocubist work is
Pavel Janák's Adria Palace. Another
vivid example is the Bank Legií by
Gočár on Na poříčí (now the Ministry
for Industry) – with a patriotic frieze
by Otto Gutfreund on the wall. Emil
Králíček's Diamant (Diamond House –
1912) on Spálená ulice offers a
coruscating display of variations on
the diamond form – not beautiful, but
undeniably arresting.

Gardens and parks

Garden culture has a long tradition in Prague and reached its apotheosis in the Baroque period. By the mid-18th century, gardens bejewelled the north slope of Petřín Hill, the slopes beneath Strahov and the southern reaches of Hradčany. In the 19th and 20th centuries, many of the city's most attractive green spaces became municipal parks.

Botanická zahrada (Botanical Garden)

Prague boasted of a botanical garden even in the 14th century. Situated where the main post office is now, it was run by a Florentine apothecary. The present garden is charming, though a bit run-down (*see p43*).
Praha 2, Na slupi 16. Tel: 224 918 970. Open: daily 10am–6pm. Trams: 18 & 24 to Botanická zahrada. A second botanical garden is located in Troja at Nádvorní 134. Open: daily 9am–6pm.

Chotkovy sady (Chotek Park)

Founded by Count Chotek in 1833 as the city's first public park, Chotek Park contains a bizarre monument to the poet Julius Zeyer (1844–1901).
Trams: 18 & 20 to Chotkovy sady.

Královská zahrada (The Royal Gardens)

Laid out in 1534, these gardens formed the first Italian Renaissance gardens of Central Europe. A report of 1650 marvels at the myriad varieties of fruit, pomegranates, figs, lemons and limes grown here, and at the tigers, lions, lynxes and bears that were kept in the menagerie.

It was here that the botanist Mathioli cultivated the first European tulips in the 16th century. At the north end of the gardens is the Belvedere (*see p34*), and on the east side you will pass the sgraffitoed Ball Game Court designed by Bonifaz Wohlmut, which was later used as a ballroom.
Open: daily Apr–Oct 10am–6pm. Admission charge.
Trams: 22 & 23 to Pražský hrad.

Palace Gardens below Prague Castle

Three gardens in Malá Strana were restored in the 1950s, and since 1989 increasing sections of the ravishing terraces below the castle have been opened to the public. The entrance is via the Kolowrat-Černín Palace, whose garden is laid out with rococo stairways, terraces, fountains and ornamental pools.

Ledeburská, Malá Pálffyovská, Velká Pálffyovská, Kolovratská and Malá Fürstenberská Gardens. Open: daily Apr & Oct 10am–6pm, May & Sept 9am–7pm, June & July 9am–9pm, Aug 9am–8pm. Admission charge.

Vojanovy sady (Vojan Park)

Tucked away in the lower part of Malá Strana is Vojan Park, former convent gardens. To the left of the entrance is a statue of St John Nepomuk standing on a fish. Another curiosity is St Elias Chapel, which is an imitation stalactite cave that has ceiling frescoes of episodes in the saint's life.

Entrance from U Lužického semináře. Metro: Malostranská.

Královská zahrada

Vrtbovská zahrada (Vrtba Gardens)

The Vrtba Gardens, among the finest of Prague's Baroque terraced gardens, are noted for Matthias Braun's statuary: an Atlas near the entrance, and Ceres and Bacchus at the lower end.

Karmelitská ulice 26. Open: daily Apr–Oct 10am–6pm.
Admission charge.
Trams: 12, 20, 22 & 23 to Malostranské náměstí.

Zahrada Kinských (Kinský Gardens)

Prince Kinský employed Franz Höhnel to lay out this park as an English landscape garden in 1825. It passed to the municipality in 1901. Kinský Gardens contain a neoclassical villa, once used by Crown Prince Rudolf and the Archduke Franz Ferdinand. Other curiosities are an 18th-century wooden church transported from a village in the Carpatho-Ukraine in 1929, and a picturesque little campanile from Moravia.

Entrance on náměstí Kinských or from Petřín through the medieval 'Hunger Wall'. Trams: 6, 9, 12, 20, 23 & 22 to Újezd.

MORE GARDENS

For **Petřín** and **Stromovka** see pp122 & 146; for the gardens of the **Lobkowicz** and **Wallenstein palaces** see pp94, 113–14 & 116–17. The castle gardens are included in the description of **Hradčany** (see pp54–5), and for those of **Letná** see pp50–51.

Walk: Letná Park and the Royal Gardens

*This walk takes you above the left bank of the Vltava, away from the bustle and pollution of the city centre, allowing you to breathe the purer air of Letná and the Královská zahrada (Royal Gardens). (*Follow orange numbers on map for route; for green numbers see Walk on pp66–7.*)*

Allow 2 hours.

Start from Čechův most (nearest tram stop: Právnická Fakulta, No 17).

1 Čechův most (Čech Bridge)

The bridge has an attractive early 20th-century design, with angels on columns at each end, sunburst-topped lamp-posts, and Art Nouveau railings.
Cross the busy nábřeží Edvarda Beneše at the far side and climb the steep, *zigzagging double flight of steps up to Letenské sady (Letná Park).*

2 Letenské sady (Letná Park)

The vantage point on the top of the steps once boasted the largest Stalin monument in the Eastern Bloc

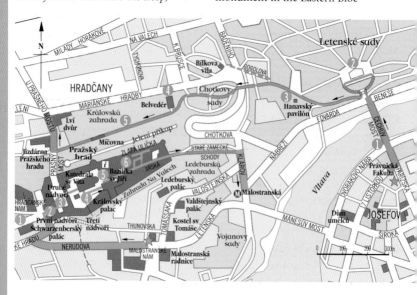

(30m/98ft high). After Khrushchev denounced Stalin, it was blown up. Where Stalin once stood, there is now a gigantic 'metronome sculpture' intended to symbolise the return to democracy. In the hillside beneath your feet is a nuclear bunker – the least-deserving members of the population planned to retire here in the event of Armageddon. It was actually used to house the city's potato supply. The view over the bridges on the Vltava and Staré Město is stunning.

3 Hanavský pavilón (Pavilion)

A short walk southwest brings you to the extravagantly ornate Hanavský pavilón, originally erected for the Paris World Exhibition of 1878, and re-erected here in 1898. It has a charming little café on the terrace, and a good, if expensive, restaurant.

Walk on south through leafy Letná until you come to the footbridge over Badeniho, beyond which the Belvedér (Belvedere Palace) can be seen, shrouded in trees at the end of an alley. A detour to the right before reaching the footbridge down Gogolova and across the junction brings you to the Bílkova vila at Mickiewiczova 1, former home and studio of František Bílek. His interesting Symbolist sculptures and the furniture he designed himself are on display.

4 Belvedér (Belvedere)

The Královský letohrádek (Summer Palace) or Belvedere (*see p34*) was built on the orders of Ferdinand I as a gift to his wife, Queen Anna. Its terrace was used by Rudolf II's Danish astronomer, Tycho Brahe. In the garden on the west side of this lovely Renaissance building is the bronze 'singing fountain', so-called because of the sound of its gently splashing water.

5 Královská zahrada (Royal Gardens)

The Royal Gardens (*see p48; open: Apr–Oct Tue–Sun 10am–6pm, admission charge*) form one of the best-kept parks of Prague. Experimental modern sculptures (said to have been personally chosen by President Havel) mingle with formal parterres, lawns and noble trees. Halfway up on the left is the Míčovna (Ball Game Court) with sgraffiti decoration on the exterior walls. Parallel to the gardens, to the southeast, is the Jelení příkop (former Deer Moat), where the kings used to corral their red deer. At the southwest end is the Lví dvůr (Lion's Court). This was once Rudolf II's menagerie, where lions and tigers were kept in cages that had to be provided with luxurious and expensive heating against the bitter Prague winters.

You leave the gardens at the west end, opposite the Baroque Jízdárna Pražského hradu (former Riding School) that is now used for exhibitions. Leaving the Prašny most ('Powder Bridge'), which leads into the castle complex on your left, turn right along U Prašného mostu for Mariánské hradby and the Nos 22 and 23 trams.

Prague lifestyle

There's little difference between young Czechs and other nationalities. With a trendy club scene (Radost FX has been voted one of the world's best clubs), cinemas, pleasantly seedy clubs in Prague 3 and a rich choice of outdoor activities, the fact that central Prague is tourist-packed and (sometimes) prohibitively expensive is not perhaps the end of the world. Many young Czechs travel abroad, something that the older generation was unable to do. For older Czechs, the good life means taking comfort in good jazz and good beer.

The city is a delight to walk around

In the city's highly democratic beer cellars, where professors sit cheek-by-jowl with bricklayers and shop assistants, men unwind after a day's work. However, many former dens have metamorphosed into more expensive wine and cocktail bars, chic cafés and tourist-magnet pubs. To find the beery haunts (badly lit), you'll need to stray from the centre. Coffee-house culture has suffered since its days of glory in the First Republic, but several old stalwarts, such as Malostranská Kavárna or Café Slavia, still manage to hold their own, while others, such as Café Montmartre, have been gloriously revived.

Despite low salaries, many Praguers own a *chata* (chalet) or *chalupa* (cottage) in the country. On summer weekends, the motorway is jammed as everyone heads out of the city for these often self-built second homes. Czechs are also zealous hikers. The areas around Prague and all the national parks are liberally signposted with routes for ramblers. Those who want to join them will find the *Praha okolí* – environs of Prague – of the *Soubor turistických* map series useful. *See also pp144–7.*

All Czechs, whether young or old, enjoy the good life

Hradčany

The term Hradčany is used to describe the whole area of the western hill above Malá Strana. It consists of Pražský hrad (the castle hill complex) and the former town of Hradčany to the west and north of it (see pp70–71), with Hradčanské náměstí (Hradčany Square, see pp68–9) as its focal point. The Pražský hrad (Prague Castle) towers over the Vltava. In the late 9th century, it was fortified by Duke Bořivoj, and has been the spiritual and political focus of the territory of the current Czech lands since.

Pražský hrad (Prague Castle)

After its diminutive and graceful beginnings in the Romanesque period (Bazilika svatého Jiří, St George's Basilica, and a rotunda Kostel svatého Víta, Church of St Vitus), the architecture of Prague Castle reached its zenith under Charles IV (1346–78), when Matthew of Arras and Petr Parléř (Peter Parler) were at work on the great Gothic cathedral. In the late 14th century, King Vladislav Jagiello commissioned the castle's finest secular architecture from Benedikt Ried – the jousting hall in the Royal Palace. The Habsburgs' architectural legacy, apart from the Belvedere and the Royal Gardens, is depressingly pervasive. The castle area was clad in a barracks-like Baroque classicism by Maria Theresa's architect, Nicolo Pacassi. The last architect of distinction to work on the buildings and gardens was Slovene Josip Plečnik, who was commissioned in the 1920s by Czechoslovakia's first president, Tomáš Masaryk, to remodel some of the Baroque features and the bastions. The castle lies at the heart of Czech consciousness and of Central European culture and history. It has seen imperial grandeur, and played host to humanist scholars, alchemists and occultists under the eccentric Rudolf II. It has been likened to Kafka's fictional castle under the Communists' rule of darkness; now it is the ceremonial residence of a democratic head of state.

První nádvoří (First Courtyard)

The tall wrought-iron gates of the entrance are topped by copies of battling Titans by the Baroque sculptor Ignaz Platzer. There is a changing of the guard every hour, from 5am to 11pm, and a solemn fanfare at noon. The noon fanfare, played from the first-floor windows, was composed by rock star Michal Kocáb, who subsequently became an MP.

Zahrada Na Baště
(Garden on the Bastion)

The entrance to the left of the main gateway leads to the Bastion Garden, remodelled by Josip Plečnik in 1927. It has two levels connected by a circular stairway. The neoclassical pavilion is by Plečnik's successor as castle architect, Otto Rottmayer.

Druhé nádvoří (Second Courtyard)

This is entered through the early Baroque **Matyášova brána (Matthias Gate)**, originally free-standing, later incorporated into Pacassi's rebuilding plan. In the north corner are the **Rudofova galerie (Rudolf Gallery)** and the **Španělský sál (Spanish Hall)**, whose sumptuous neo-Baroque interiors are not normally open to the public, although classical concerts are held in the latter. From the northern exit of the

CASTLE INFORMATION

Pražský hrad, *119 08 Praha I, Hradčany*. The courtyards and streets of Castle Hill are open until late evening. Sites with a ticket required are open 9am–5pm daily. *The castle building is open: daily 5am–midnight; gardens open: Apr–Oct 5am–midnight, Nov–Mar 5am–11pm.* The **Information Office** is in the third courtyard (*tel: 224 373 368*). Tickets can be bought here and guided tours arranged. *www.hrad.cz*

castle, access is gained to **Obrazárna Pražského hradu (Castle Gallery)**, containing the remnants of Rudolf II's art collection. This outstanding collection once consisted of 3,000 pictures and 2,500 sculptures, but most of it was looted by the Swedes in 1648. Joseph II sold off much of the rest (Titian's *Leda and the Swan* was listed in the inventory as *Nude Being Bitten by an Angry Goose*). Among the remains is a

Hradčany

Count the steps to Hradčany, which rises above Malá Strana

Bronze sculptures adorning St Vitus Cathedral

bust of Rudolf by Adrian de Vries, and works by Titian, Guido Reni and Rubens. *Castle Gallery open: daily 10am–6pm. Admission charge.*

Kaple svatého Kříže (Chapel of the Holy Cross)

The building in the southeast corner is Anselmo Lurago's Chapel of the Holy Cross, given its neoclassical aspect when it was altered in the 19th century. Formerly the Treasury, it has become a somewhat dreary art gallery.

Katedrála svatého Víta (St Vitus Cathedral)

The earliest church on the site of St Vitus (third courtyard of Prague Castle) was a small Romanesque rotunda, founded by Duke (later St) Wenceslas around 925. The choice of St Vitus as the church's dedicatee may have been connected with the fact that the similarly sounding pagan god 'Svantovit' was previously worshipped here. Wenceslas also received a valuable

propaganda boost for the new sanctuary in the form of St Vitus arm, donated by the King of Saxony. Four centuries later Charles IV was able to secure the rest of St Vitus for his treasury. This was a major coup, for the cult of this highly prophylactic saint (invoked against epilepsy and 'St Vitus dance' or chorea) was hugely popular in the Middle Ages.

In 1039 the bones of the most important local martyr, St Adalbert, were also placed in the rotunda. It thus became a much-frequented pilgrimage shrine; so much so that a larger church had to be built in 1060 – a towered Romanesque basilica dedicated to Sts Vitus, Adalbert and Wenceslas, whose tombs were inside. Some remains of the original rotunda and basilica came to light in the 1920s as the cathedral was undergoing its last phase of building. *www.katedralapraha.cz. Open: Mar–Oct Mon–Sat 9am–5pm, Sun noon–5pm, Nov–Feb Mon–Sat 9am–4pm, Sun noon–4pm. Admission charge.*

The building of the Gothic cathedral

When Prague became an archbishopric in 1344, the future Charles IV summoned Matthew of Arras from Avignon to build a cathedral in the severe Gothic style of contemporary church architecture in France. When he died in 1352, he had completed eight chapels. In 1356 Petr Parléř, a Swabian, took over the work, and it is to his genius that we owe the altogether overwhelming power and beauty of St Vitus architecture. In particular, it is his vision that produced the striking contrast between the complex ornateness of the exterior walls and the calm immensity of the interior.

By 1366 Parléř had completed the Chapel of St Wenceslas. The choir was consecrated in 1385, at which time a 'temporary' wall was erected between it and the nave (which was still under construction). Little did the optimistic builders imagine that this wall would still be in place nearly five centuries later!

Parléř and his workshop began the triforium, with its busts of dynastic and other figures, and laid the foundation stone for the great South Tower in 1392. After he died in 1399, his sons Wenceslas and John worked on for 20 years.

The Hussite wars (*see p39*) brought building to a halt, but there was a final phase of Gothic construction under King Vladislav Jagiello, whose architect designed the unusual Royal Oratory, built in the 1480s.

In 1843 the Association for the Completion of St Vitus Cathedral was set up to raise funds. In the second half of the 19th century, Josef Mocker carried through plans that respected the spirit of Parléř's Gothic design, but also managed to salvage important Renaissance and Baroque features that had been added over the years. Work continued into the 20th century, and it was not until the 1929 millennial anniversary commemoration of the murder of St Wenceslas that the entire church was completed and finally dedicated.

The Gothic St Vitus Cathedral, Prague's largest church

Entrance, spire and stairway

On entering the third courtyard of the castle you are confronted with the cathedral's main entrance in its neo-Gothic western section, but walk round to the south side to admire Petr Parléř's fine architecture. He built the Gothic part of the 96m (315ft) high bell tower, which is topped by a Renaissance gallery and Pacassi's Baroque spire. To the right is the triple-arched Golden Portal, and, higher up, a remarkable openwork stairway which is a good example of the unconventional boldness of Parléř's design.

Kaple svatého Václava
(St Wenceslas Chapel)

Immediately on your right as you enter through the south portal is the chapel built to hold the remains of Bohemia's most beloved patron saint. Some 1,370 precious stones are set in its lower walls, perhaps signifying the year it was

ST WENCESLAS

The door of the chapel has a lion's-head knocker to which, it is claimed, the dying Wenceslas clung when struck down by his brother Boleslav. The murder took place 20km (12 miles) outside Prague at Stará Boleslav. The motives for the killing appear to have been dynastic and political rather than religious; nevertheless, Wenceslas was treated as a martyr. His remains were subsequently transferred to St Vitus apparently by a repentant Boleslav. J M Neale's famous carol (which promotes Duke Wenceslas to king) is unhistorical, although the image of him as a just and merciful ruler may have had some substance.

completed. Frescoes depict the New Heavenly Jerusalem, the Life of Wenceslas and the Passion of Our Lord; there is also a statue of the saint by Parléř's nephew Heinrich, and the (much-restored) Wenceslas tomb. The crown jewels are kept above the chapel but are seldom on view to the public.

Panel reliefs

In the north ambulatory, opposite Parléř's Old Sacristy, is a finely carved oak panel with a relief depicting the Elector Frederick's retreat from Prague after the defeat of the Bohemian Protestants at the White Mountain. A complementary panel in the south ambulatory shows Protestants plundering the cathedral in 1619.

The Royal Oratory

Beyond the two chapels to the east of the St Wenceslas Chapel is the Royal Oratory, a hanging vault with intricate Gothic decoration which resembles the branches of a tree. Designed for King Vladislav Jagiello, it was connected with the king's bedroom in the palace by a covered gangway. The Baroque figure on the left-hand edge represents a miner from the silver mines at Kutná Hora (*see pp140–41*).

The Tomb of St John Nepomuk

Two chapels further on is the Baroque tomb of St John Nepomuk by Fischer von Erlach the Younger (1736). The cherub on the lid is pointing to the saint's tongue, a reference to the Jesuit claim that this part of his remains had never decayed. (According to legend the saint refused to betray the secrets of the queen's confession to Wenceslas IV.)

Other sights of interest
In the centre of the cathedral is the Royal Mausoleum, a fine Renaissance work with reliefs of Bohemian kings. Next to it is the entrance to the crypt, and archaeological remains of the two earlier churches on this site. The third chapel from the west end on the north wall contains Alphonse Mucha's stained-glass window of Sts Cyril and Methodius. Next to it is František Bílek's remarkable *Crucifixion* (1899).

Finally, it is worth taking binoculars to see the 21 sandstone busts by the Parléř school high up in the triforium.

One of the imposing portals of St Vitus Cathedral

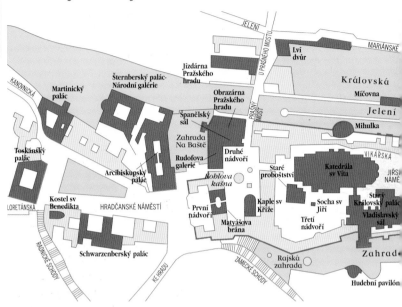

Zahrada Na Baště

Toskánský palác

Martinický palác

Šternberský palác-Národní galérie

Jízdárna Pražského hradu

Obrazárna Pražského hradu

Španělský sál

Rudofova galerie

Druhé nádvoří

Arcibiskupský palác

Kohlova kašna

Kostel sv Benedikta

HRADČANSKÉ NÁMĚSTÍ

První nádvoří

Matyášova brána

Schwarzenberský palác

Staré probošství

Kaple sv Kříže

Socha sv Jiří

Třetí nádvoří

Katedrála sv Víta

Lví dvůr

MARIÁNSKÉ

Královská

Míčovna

Jelení

Mihulka

VIKÁŘSKÁ

JIRSKÉ NÁMĚSTÍ

Starý Královský palác

Vladislavský sál

Rajská zahrada

Zahrad

Hudební pavilón

Zahrada Na Valech (Rampart Garden)

On the south side of the third courtyard, a flight of steps gives access to the Rampart Garden with a viewing terrace by Josip Plečnik (1924). At the west end it merges with the Rajská zahrada (Paradise Garden), changed by Plečnik, but originally laid out in 1562.

Starý královský palác (Old Royal Palace)

On the southeast side of the third courtyard is the entrance to the Royal

The vaulted ceiling of the Vladislav Hall

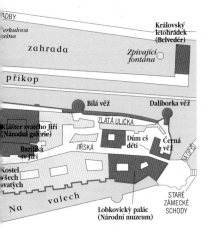

Palace of the Bohemian rulers between the 11th and 16th centuries. The top part was chiefly built by Benedikt Rejt for King Vladislav Jagiello in the 15th century. Ried was responsible for the **Vladislavský sál (Vladislav Hall)**, entered from the antechamber. On the way, note the Green Room to your left, once the Supreme Court, and Vladislav's Bedchamber. This great space (16m/52ft wide, 62m/203ft long, 13m/43ft high) was constructed between 1493 and 1502 in the late-Gothic style as a jousting and banqueting hall. In Rudolf II's time, the space was used as a bazaar and, since 1918, the presidents of the republic have been sworn in here.

Light streams in from the huge Renaissance windows on either side.

The door in the southwest corner gives access to the Bohemian Chancellery in the Louis Wing of the palace, scene of the third Prague defenestration in 1618. After returning to the Vladislav Hall, walk to the far end where there is a viewing platform offering fine views over Prague. At the east end of the hall is the rather dreary **Kostel Všech svatých (All Saints' Chapel)**. More interesting is the **Hall of the Diet** in the northeast corner, the work of Bonifaz Wohlmut (1563). Portraits of 18th- and 19th-century Habsburgs adorn the walls. To the left is the Riders' Staircase, up which the knights rode to their tournaments in the great hall. At the bottom are the earlier Gothic and Romanesque parts of the palace, where copies of some of the busts on the triforium of St Vitus are displayed, and where visitors will find the 'Story of Prague Castle' exhibition. *Open: daily Apr–Oct 9am–6pm, Nov–Mar 9am–4pm. Admission charge.*

Outside St George's Basilica

Jiřské náměstí

Leaving the Royal Palace by the Riders' Staircase you enter Jiřské náměstí (St George's Square).

Klášter svatého Jiří (Convent of St George)

In the northeast corner of the square is the Convent of St George. Its foundation in 973 marked the elevation of Prague to a bishopric, and its first abbess was Mlada, sister of the then ruler, Boleslav II. It remained a convent for Benedictine nuns until Joseph II turned it into barracks in 1782. Since 1972 it has housed the National Gallery's collection of early Czech art and Gothic panel paintings. (*See p110.*)

Jiřske náměstí 33.
Tel: 257 531 644. www.ngprague.cz.
Open: daily 10am–6pm.
Admission charge.

BOHEMIA'S FIRST MARTYR

Duke Wenceslas' grandmother Ludmila was bitterly resented by his mother Drahomira for her influence over her grandson. Ludmila was forced to retire from Prague to Tetín near Karlštejn, where she was murdered by Drahomira's mercenaries in September 921. Over her grave a church was built dedicated to the Archangel Michael, so that all miracles that occurred could be ascribed to him instead.

In 925 Wenceslas had the remains of his grandmother brought to Prague and ceremonially deposited in St George's Basilica. They proved to be undecayed, and even gave off an agreeable odour, two indisputable indications of saintliness.

Bazilika svatého Jiří
(Basilica of St George)

Adjoining the convent to the south is the Basilica of St George. Restoration at the turn of the 20th century and in the 1960s has made this Prague's best-preserved Romanesque building, although it has inevitably lost some of its ancient lustre. Inside there are three aisles, the middle one a great, barn-like hall with a flat wooden ceiling. At the east end a triumphal arch frames a raised altar approached by a double flight of Baroque steps. In front of the steps are the tombs of Boleslav II and Duke Vratislav (the founder of the church), and between them is the entrance to the 12th-century crypt.

The origins of the church go back to the early history of Prague, to the beginning of the 10th century. The last alterations were carried out in 1680, when the chapel of St John Nepomuk was built at the southwest end and the somewhat incongruous Baroque façade was added.

At the southeast end is the chapel dedicated to St Ludmila, Bohemia's first martyr. It contains her tomb, designed by Petr Parléř, and frescoes by J V Hellich (1858) depicting her life and martyrdom.

Open: daily 9am–5pm (4pm in winter). Admission charge.

Lobkovický palác
(Lobkovic Palace)

South of the basilica at Jiřská ulice No 1 is the former seat of the Lobkowiczes, who were fervent protagonists of the Counter-Reformation. In 1618 the redoubtable Polyxena of Lobkovic took in the two councillors ejected by Protestant nobles from a Chancellery window, and refused entry to their pursuers. Two floors of the palace are given over to a museum of Czech history.

Jiřská ulice 3. Tel: 257 534 578. Open: daily 10.30am–6pm. Admission charge.

Inside St George's Basilica

The diminutive houses of Golden Lane

Zlatá ulička (Golden Lane)

At the north end of the castle complex (approached from the rear of St George's Convent) is Golden Lane. The emperor's 24 gatekeepers originally lived in its little houses, pursuing various crafts and trades to eke out their miserable wages. Later, goldsmiths and other artisans arrived. The Renaissance house backing on to the south side of the lane belonged to the *burgrave* (the king's deputy).

No 22, which was occupied by Franz Kafka in 1916–17, now belongs to the Kafka Society. Nobel Prize-winning poet Jaroslav Seifert also lived in Golden Lane.

Prašná věž – Mihulka (Powder Tower or Mihulka)

At the western end of Golden Lane is the Powder Tower, part of the 13th-century castle fortifications and, later, where Rudolf II's alchemists laboured to find the formula for making gold. Among those who worked on this doomed project were the Englishmen John Dee (formerly employed by Elizabeth I) and Edward Kelley. They were both later disgraced for failing to deliver the goods. Kelley was to end up a prisoner in the castle of Křivoklát (*see p139*). On display are the alchemists' equipment and a bell foundry.

The name 'Mihulka' apparently refers to the lampreys (*mihule*) bred here for the royal kitchens.

Open: daily Apr–Oct 9am–6pm, Nov–Mar 9am–4pm. Admission charge.

Daliborka věž (Dalibor Tower)

This tower, built in 1436 by Benedikt Rejt at the east end of the lane, was used as a jail until the end of the 18th century. It takes its name from the nobleman imprisoned there in 1498 on suspicion of aiding and abetting a peasants' revolt near Leitmeritz. Legend says he passed the days before his execution playing the violin so movingly that passers-by filled the basket he let down from his window with victuals and money. Bedřich Smetana used the story for one of his best-known operas, *Dalibor*.

Closed to visitors.

Bílá věž (White Tower) and Černá věž (Black Tower)

The White Tower (midway along Golden Lane) and the Black Tower at the eastern tip of the castle were prisons, the latter for debtors. The legend goes that the 16th-century aristocrat Katharine Lažan died in the White Tower, accused of having murdered several young female servants in order to retain her beauty by washing in their maidenly blood.

You can stroll along the passage linking the towers, with arrow-slit views, and lined with lurid shields and heavy suits of armour.

A massive stone gateway leads from Charles Bridge to Malá Strana

Walk: A stroll around Castle Hill

Pražský hrad (Prague Castle) was the spiritual and political focus of the city for most of its history. There has been a fortress and a church here since the 9th century. A detailed description of the buildings is given on pages 54–65 (see green numbers on map on p50 for the route). If you want to take just a short stroll, allow about an hour; comprehensive sightseeing requires at least half a day, if not more.

Approach Hradčany up Nerudova and Ke Hradu from Malostranské náměstí (trams 12, 20, 22 & 23).

1 Hradčanské náměstí

Hradčany Square (*see pp68–9*) is flanked by noble buildings such as the Arcibiskupský palác (Archbishop's Palace) on the north side. Its late incumbent, the heroic Cardinal Tomášek, lived just long enough to see the collapse of the godless regime he withstood. Karl Schwarzenberg, the scion of the former owners of the Schwarzenberský palác (Schwarzenberg Palace) on the south side, enjoyed a remarkable tenure as personal adviser to President Havel. Havel's influence is clearly visible in the uniforms of the guards on duty below the statues of battling giants atop the first gateway. The costume designer for Miloš Forman's film *Amadeus* was commissioned by the president to design the Ruritanian outfits.

2 První nádvoří

The two huge flagstaffs in the První nádvoří (First Courtyard) are made from fir trees, and date from the remodelling of the castle area by the Slovene architect Josip Plečnik during the First Republic. Ahead you can see the plain Baroque façade of the Presidential Apartments (to the south), and (to the north) the Spanish Hall and Castle Gallery. All this, together with the east wing of the next courtyard, is the work of Maria Theresa's architect, Nicolo Pacassi.
Pass through the Matthias Gate.

3 Druhé nádvoří

The Matyášova brána (Matthias Gate), leading to the Druhé nádvoří (Second Courtyard), is a triumphal arch named after the brother of Rudolf II. The neoclassical building on the right is the Kaple svatého Kříže (Chapel of the Holy Cross), once the treasury, now a gallery.

4 Třetí nádvoří

The Třetí nádvoří (Third Courtyard), beyond, is dominated by the Katedrála svatého Víta (Cathedral of St Vitus). Walk across the space to get a better view of the South Tower, and the early Gothic architecture of the eastern end of this great edifice constructed by Petr Parléř and his sons. If you walk on through the courtyard, the Královský palác (Old Royal Palace), with its celebrated Vladislavský sál (Vladislav Hall) and Riders' Staircase, is ahead of you. On the right, Plečnik's green cylindrical canopy entices you down some steps to the Rampart Gardens.
Enter U Sv Jiří.

5 Bazilika svatého Jiří

The last courtyard – St George's Square – contains the Basilica of St George, one of the finest surviving Romanesque buildings in Central Europe. The origins of this and the adjacent monastery lie in the 10th century. The basilica regularly hosts chamber music concerts. The monastery houses the National Gallery's collection of early Bohemian art.
Now take Jiřská, beside the church, and turn left as soon as you can to reach the famous Zlatá ulička (Golden Lane).

6 Zlatá ulička

In the 19th century, the tiny 16th-century houses that line the street were supposed to have been the dwellings of Rudolf II's alchemists. Franz Kafka also lived here for a while. Prepare to find the lane densely packed with tourists.
Return to Jiřská and descend the steps at the eastern tip of Castle Hill, which lead eventually to Klárov, the Malostranská metro station and the No 22 tram.

The castle complex lies at the heart of the city

Hradčanské náměstí

Hradčany Square

The township of Hradčany dates back to 1320 and originally consisted of little more than the square itself (see p54 & below). Following a devastating fire in 1541, most of the burghers' houses were pulled down by the Catholic nobility, who bought up large plots and built great palaces on them. In the centre of the square is Ferdinand Brokoff's Marian Column (1726).

Schwarzenberský palác (Schwarzenberg Palace)

At No 2 on the south side of the square, the Schwarzenberg Palace has a number of striking Italianate features, including Lombardy cornices and Renaissance sgraffiti. When Agostino Galli originally built it for the Lobkowiczes in 1563, seven existing houses on the site had to be demolished. Inside (on the second floor) are exquisitely detailed tempera frescoes depicting scenes from Homer.

The Schwarzenbergs acquired the building only in 1719. A previous owner became famous for having invited Tycho Brahe (the imperial mathematician) to a party in 1601. It proved to be his last outing: according to the story, as a result of overindulgence at dinner, his bladder burst on the way home.

Having undergone extensive renovation, this magnificent building now houses the National Gallery's exhibition of Baroque art in Bohemia.

Open: Tue–Sun 10am–6pm. Admission charge.

Arcibiskupský palác (Archbishop's Palace)

Close to the castle's gates is the Archbishop's Palace at No 16, boasting an elegant rococo façade by Johan Wirch (1764). Traces of Jean-Baptiste Mathey's earlier Baroque design (1676) may be seen in the entrance portals and the tympanum rising above the middle of the façade. With this first commission in Prague, Mathey introduced many of the architectural principles of the Italian Baroque he had learnt in Rome.

The original Renaissance palace on this site was presented by Ferdinand I to the first post-Hussite archbishop of Prague, whose residence thus moved closer to the centre of power at Pražský hrad. Bonifaz Wohlmut had it rebuilt in 1564.

The palace is open to the public only once a year on Maundy Thursday from 9am–5pm.

Šternberský palác (Sternberg Palace)

The left-hand entrance arch of the Archbishop's Palace leads to the Sternberg Palace, at No 15, a building of the high Baroque designed by Giovanni Alliprandi. The Chinoiserie room on the second floor is notable, but the main reason for visiting the palace is the National Gallery's collection of old European art (*see p110*).

Open: Tue–Sun 10am–6pm.
Tel: 220 514 634.

Martinický palác (Martinic Palace)

Restoration during 1971 brought to light sgraffiti depicting the story of Joseph and Potiphar on the impressive Renaissance façade of the Martinic Palace (No 8). Its owner from 1624 was Jaroslav Bořita of Martinitz, one of the councillors defenestrated from the Bohemian Chancellery in 1618. He was later made a count for his troubles. Both he and his fellow victim, Vilém Slavata, arranged to have their miraculous escape immortalised in bombastic sculptures for their palaces.

The palace is not open to the public.

Toskánský palác (Tuscany Palace)

This huge and rather sombre palace, at the west end of the square (No 5), was built by Jean-Baptiste Mathey in 1689–91, and owned by the Dukes of Tuscany between 1718 and 1918. It now belongs to the Czech Foreign Ministry.

Hradčanské náměstí

Renaissance sgraffiti on the Schwarzenberg Palace

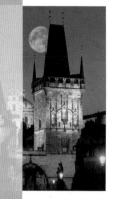

Walk: Hradčany hinterland

The tranquil backwater of the castle district seems frozen in time. The bustling medieval town fell victim to the great fire of 1541, but in the 17th century the Catholic beneficiaries of the Counter-Reformation built grandiose palaces which still abound.

Allow 2¹/₂ hours.

The walk begins in Hradčanské náměstí, reached via Nerudova and Ke Hradu from Malostranské náměstí.

1 Hradčanské náměstí

Apart from the Arcibiskupský palác (Archbishop's Palace) and the Schwarzenberský palác (Schwarzenberg Palace – *see p68*), the western end of the square is dominated by the Toskánský palác (Tuscany Palace). North of it, on the corner of Kanovnická, is the more modest Martinický palác (Martinic Palace), notable for its lively sgraffito decoration. In the centre of the square is a Baroque Marian column, erected in thanksgiving for deliverance from the plague. Also worth a look is the heavily ornate wrought-iron street lamp, one of two in Prague.
Walk west along Loretánská, and turn right down to the shrine of Loreta.

2 The Loreta

The Loreta is inspired by the famous Italian original (Loreto) that claims to possess the Santa Casa, the house in Nazareth where the Annunciation took place. The most entertaining part is the cloisters, lined with saints whose responsibilities range from curing gallstones (St Liborius) to the return of lost property (St Anthony). The Church of the Nativity is notable for the depiction of St Agatha carrying her severed breasts on a plate, and the treasury for an outrageously over-the-top diamond monstrance designed by Fischer von Erlach. (*See also pp72–3.*)
Walk back up to the junction with Pohořelec and turn right.

3 Černínský palác

On the corner is the vast, rusticated façade of the Černín Palace, the largest in Prague. During the First Republic, it was taken over by the Foreign Ministry and it was from here that Jan Masaryk, the only non-Communist left in the cabinet of Klement Gottwald, plunged to his death in suspicious circumstances on 10 March 1948.
Continue down Pohořelec, passing the junction with Úvoz, then turn left into a cobbled square, around which are the buildings of Strahovský klášter (see p74).

4 Strahovský klášter

This is the home of Premonstratensian monks and was founded in 1140. The high point of any visit is the frescoed library, particularly the Philosophical Hall with its painted ceiling (*The History of Humanity*) by Franz Anton Maulpertsch.
Leave the monastery by an archway in the eastern wall and walk south through the Strahov Gardens. The Vltava and Malá Strana unfold before you. In two minutes you see steps to your left, which lead up to Petřín (see below and p122).

5 Petřín

This is an especially pleasant part of the walk, winding through pear and plum orchards. At the top of the crumbling steps is Prague's mini-Eiffel Tower. Nearby are the Bludiště (Mirror Maze) and the Observatory.

Some say it is said to have been built as a job-creation scheme by Charles IV between 1360 and 1362; others point out that it was paid for by the expropriation of the Jews.

The funicular railway (*lanová dráha*) terminus on the summit is approached through a rose garden. The railway is now electric, but until the 1960s it was worked by water pressure. Petřín Hill features in the short story *The Great Wall of China* by Franz Kafka.
Descend to Újezd, where you can pick up trams to the city centre.

Walk: Hradčany hinterland

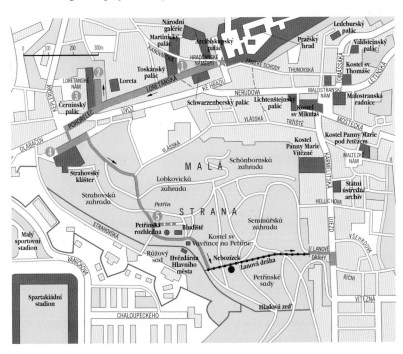

AROUND HRADČANY
The Loreta

After the Catholic victory at the battle of the White Mountain (1620), the Czech lands were swept by a wave of pietism. To eradicate nostalgia for Protestant heresies and heroes, the formidable propaganda machine of the Counter-Reformation was turned up full blast. In particular, the Marian cult was exploited, replacing Protestant hostility to images with a mixture of symbolism, sensuality and superstition.

Mariolatry was given its first major impetus in Bohemia with the founding of the Prague Loreto by the Spanish-born Benigna Kateřina Lobkowicz in 1626. The focus of the sanctuary was an imitation of the Santa Casa, claimed to be the historical house of the Virgin Mary, originally in Nazareth, but deposited by angels on Italian shores in a laurel grove (*loreto*) near Ancona. This legend appealed to public imagination: countless 'Loretos' sprang up in Catholic Europe, and eventually there were some 50 in Bohemia alone.

The west façade

Designed by Christoph Dientzenhofer, the outer wing was completed by his son Kilián in 1726. The rich decoration on the façade is crowned by a kneeling Virgin Mary (above the left-hand gable), and by the Angel of the Annunciation (over the right-hand gable). Below are the four Evangelists and St Christopher. The coat of arms of the shrine's patrons,

Baroque tower above the Loreta shrine

Prince Philipp Lobkowicz and his wife, is above the entrance.

The clock tower

A carillon in the clock tower plays the Marian hymn 'We Greet Thee a Thousand Times' every hour on the hour. The mechanism was made in Amsterdam and consists of 27 bells collectively weighing about 1,600kg (3,500lbs).

The astronomer Tycho Brahe successfully petitioned Rudolf II to order the monks to ring their evensong carillon before it got dark, as otherwise it disturbed his concentration when stargazing!

The cloisters

The lower arcade has an upper storey added by Kilián Dientzenhofer in the

1740s. The painted ceilings of the vaults feature motifs from the litany used during processions at Loreto itself. The arcades themselves are lined with beautiful representations of saints with miraculous healing powers, whose fields of expertise are inscribed below their statues. Thus, a sore throat falls under the ambit of St Blaise, toothache will be treated by St Apollonia and plague by St Roch.

Kostel Narození Páně (Church of the Nativity)

On the east side of the sanctuary this 18th-century church has a fine fresco of *Christ in the Temple* by Václav Reiner. Other frescoes by J V Schöpf depict the Christmas scene of the *Three Kings and the Shepherds*.

The Santa Casa

In the middle of the cloisters is the Santa Casa, the spiritual focus of the Loreta, built by Giovanni Orsi and Andrea Allio in 1631. Rich stucco depicts figures from the Old Testament and scenes from the life of the Virgin. A limewood statue of Our Lady encased in elaborate silver decoration glimmers in the dim religious light.

The treasury

On the first floor is the fabulous treasury, whose loveliest work is a diamond monstrance (1699), designed by Johann Fischer von Erlach and made by Viennese silversmiths. The dramatic and sensual representation of the joint victory of Maria Immaculata and the Trinity over the forces of evil is a stunning example of Baroque extravagance. It is said that many of its 6,222 diamonds came from the court dress of the benefactress Countess Kolowrat, who left her entire fortune to the Loreta.

Loretánské náměstí (Hradčany).
Tel: 220 516 740. www.loreta.cz.
Open: Tue–Sun 9am–noon, 1–4.30pm.
Admission charge.
Trams: 22 & 23 to Pohořelec.

Old Town Prague is a magnificent symphony of spires and towers

Strahovský klášter (Strahov Monastery)

Strahov owes its name to its commanding position on Charles IV's city fortification (*strahovní* means 'to watch over'). The monastery (*see p71*) is approached either from Pohořelec No 8, up narrow steps or through a Baroque archway further east. The arch is crowned with J A Quittainer's statue of St Norbert, founder of the Premonstratensian Order that occupied the monastery after its foundation by Prince Vladislav II in 1140. In 1627, the monks acquired the remains of the saint.

In the courtyard you will pass the deconsecrated **Kostel svatého Rocha** (**Church of St Rock**), erected by Rudolf II in gratitude to the saint for his efforts

Baroque ornamentation on the Troja Palace

in ensuring that Prague was spared the 1599 plague epidemic. Beyond is the **Kostel Nanebevzetí Panny Marie** (**Church of the Assumption**). Quittainer's impressive *Immaculata* over the portal provides a foretaste of the rich Baroque interior. Mozart twice played on the church's mighty organ, which has 4,000 pipes and 63 stops.

Nearby is a ticket office for visits to Strahov's most spectacular sights, the **Teologický sál** (**Theological Hall**) and the **Filozofický sál** (**Philosophical Hall**), both libraries. The Theological Hall was built in 1671 with a pleasing barrelled vault by Giovanni Orsi. One of the monks, Siard Nosecký, painted frescoes illustrating man's struggle to acquire wisdom. A similar theme forms the leitmotif of the neighbouring Philosophical Hall, where the ceiling was painted by the great Viennese-trained master Franz Anton Maulpertsch in 1784. His *Struggle of Mankind to Know Real Wisdom* boldly includes pre-Christian figures, such as Alexander the Great, Aristotle, Plato, Socrates and Diogenes the Cynic (sitting in his barrel). *Strahovské nádvoří 1/132, Hradčany. Tel: 220 517 208. Open: daily 9am–noon, 1–5pm. Tram: 22 or 23 to Pohořelec. Strahov also houses the Památník národního písemnictví (National Literature Museum).*

Trojský zámek (Troja Palace)

The red-and-white-painted Troja Palace in Prague 7 is a splendid architectural homage to victory, commissioned by

Theological Hall in the Strahov Monastery, with its magnificent ceiling frescoes

Habsburg loyalist Count Wenceslas Šternberk just after the spectacular defeat of the Turkish armies at the gates of Vienna in 1683. Jean-Baptiste Mathey designed the summer palace with formal French gardens. The grand steps on the garden side are embellished with statues representing the battle between Gods and Titans. In the Great Hall, busts of Habsburg emperors line the wall in the Roman manner, and a huge mural by Dutch artist Abraham Godin shows the triumphal procession of Leopold I after the Turks had been put to flight.

The palace is now administered by the Museum of the City of Prague, and contains a good display of Czech 19th-century painting.

Prague 7, U trojského zámku 1, Troja. Tel: 283 851 614. Open: Apr–Oct Tue–Sun 10am–6pm; Nov–Mar Sat & Sun 10am–5pm. Gardens open: Tue–Sun 10am–5pm all year.

Admission charge for palace.

Metro: Nádraží Holešovice, then bus 112 to Zoologiká zahrada.

Josefov

The Jews started arriving in Prague in the 10th century and settled on both sides of the Vltava. Their first eviction was at the hands of Otakar II, who needed their land for his new town on the west bank. From that time until the deportations to concentration camps under the Nazis, theirs was a history of recurrent victimisation and violence. Now only about 2,000 Jews are said to live in Prague.

The two worst pogroms of the Middle Ages were in 1086, when the Crusaders indulged in an orgy of Jew-killing, and 1389, when 3,000 Jews were massacred over Easter. In 1745 Maria Theresa

Inside the Spanish Synagogue

expelled the Jewish population from Prague, but had to allow them back soon afterwards under pressure from commercial interests. Joseph II's 'Edict of Tolerance' in 1781 somewhat improved their lot, but with the rise of Czech nationalism in the 19th century, many German-speaking Jews found themselves on the wrong side of the cultural divide. Nevertheless, in the first half of the 20th century, German Jewish literary culture flourished, producing a string of major writers including Franz Kafka, Max Brod, Egon Erwin Kisch and Franz Werfel.

All that ended with the Nazis, who killed 80,000 of the 90,000 Jews who remained in Bohemia after the invasion. A grotesque footnote to the genocide was Hitler's decision to found, in Prague, a Jewish Museum which he designated an 'Exotic Museum of an Extinct Race'.

Josefov is reached by metro to Staroměstská or tram 17. See Walk on pp80–81.

Universal symbol of Judaism

The ghetto

The ghetto was built in the 13th century in accordance with the Church's view that Jewish dwellings should be kept separate from those of Christians. From time to time, ordinances regarding clothing – designed to mark out Jews – were promulgated. Under Vratislav II they had to wear yellow cloaks; later it was bizarre hats or yellow circles.

Under Rudolf II, whose financial adviser was the Jew Mordechai Maisel, the Jewish community achieved a greater degree of autonomy. The emperor's obsession with the occult also engendered an interest in cabbalistic lore and learning (this was the age of Rabbi Jehuda Löw, credited with creating the 'Golem' – *see p78*).

In 1784 Jewish residence restrictions were abolished following Joseph II's Edict, but by the end of the 19th century the ghetto area had become an insanitary slum and red-light district. In 1893 many buildings were razed to make way for a modern quarter.

ŽIDOVSKÉ MUZEUM V PRAZE (PRAGUE JEWISH MUSEUM)

A single ticket covers access to all the sights of the State Jewish Museum listed below, and includes admission to the Robert Guttmann Gallery. The Old-New Synagogue does not form part of the museum.

Office and Jewish museum: U Staré Školy 1. Tel: 221 711 511. www.jewishmuseum.cz Sights open: Sun–Fri, Nov–Mar 9am–4.30pm, Apr–Oct 9am–6pm. Admission charge. Tickets available from the Klausová Synagóga on U starého hřbitova. Last tickets are issued half an hour before closing time. Most monuments close over lunch, noon–1pm.

Klausová synagoga (Klaus Synagogue)

This 17th-century building houses a permanent exhibition of Jewish customs and traditions. Rabbi Löw is said to have had his school here.
U starého hřbitova 4.

Maiselová synagoga (Maisel Synagogue)

Mordechai Maisel gave 12,000 denars for the construction of the synagogue in 1590. This was destroyed by fire and replaced with a new Gothic synagogue, which now houses an exhibition of the History of the Jews in Bohemia and Moravia from the 10th to the 18th centuries.
Maiselova 10.

Obřadní síň (Ceremonial Hall)

This neo-Romanesque building at the Old Jewish Cemetery entrance exhibits Jewish customs and traditions. Some 15,000 Jewish children were held here by the Nazis before being deported to Auschwitz, where the majority perished.
U starého hřbitova.

THE GOLEM LEGEND

In 1580, when the perennial accusations of ritual murders and other crimes were being levelled at the Jews, Rabbi Löw decided that the ghetto needed reassurance and protection. Using his cabbalistic knowledge (so the story goes) he was able to create a humanoid from the mud of the Vltava, the 'Golem' (Hebrew for 'unformed matter'). Its job was to act as servant and bodyguard to the community: when not required, it was switched off by placing a secret formula (*shem*) in its mouth. Like many a later Frankenstein's monster, the Golem finally escaped the control of its creator and ran amok in the rabbi's house (Löw had forgotten to put the *shem* in his mouth). For this rebellion, the humanoid was promptly turned back into a lump of clay and deposited in the attic of the Old-New Synagogue.

Pinkasova synagoga (Pinkas Synagogue)

A Rabbi Pinkas founded the earliest synagogue on this site in 1479; the Gothic vault of the interior was built in 1535, and the women's gallery was added a century later. On its walls are inscribed the names of 77,297 Bohemian and Moravian victims of the Holocaust, as well as drawings of children from the Terezín cencentration camp.
Široká 5.

Španělská synagoga (Spanish Synagogue)

The Spanish Synagogue is an Alhambra-like building with neo-Renaissance features, the work of Ignaz Ullmann (1864). It contains a history of the Jews of Bohemia and Moravia from their emancipation to the present day.
Vězeňská 1.

Staronová synagoga
(Old-New Synagogue)

Built between 1270 and 1280 and still in use, this is the most impressive of Josefov's synagogues. The design incorporates an unusual five-ribbed vaulting inside. In the vestibule are chests placed for the collection of taxes. Over the entrance to the hall is a relief of a vine with 12 bunches of grapes, supposedly representing the 12 tribes of Israel. Inside are the *almemor* (a pulpit behind a Gothic lattice) and a shrine for the Torah (a parchment scroll of the Pentateuch). A magnificent statue of Moses by František Bílek stands next to the synagogue in a small park.
Červená ulice. www.synagogue.cz.

Open: daily except Sat & Jewish holidays, Apr–Oct 9am–6pm, Nov–Mar 9.30am–4.30pm. Admission charge.

Starý židovský hřbitov
(Old Jewish Cemetery)

Over 550 years the remains of some 100,000 people have been bundled into 12 layers of graves in the Old Jewish Cemetery (*see p80*). The earliest grave is that of poet Avigdor Kara, who survived and chronicled the 1389 pogrom. Also interred here is Mordechai Maisel, who amassed 17,000 gulden from trade monopolies under Rudolf II, and was the ghetto's greatest benefactor. Rabbi Löw's tomb is sprinkled with pebbles,
(*Cont. on p84*)

Gravestones mark some of the thousands of burials at the Old Jewish Cemetery

Walk: Josefov

This walk covers the former Jewish ghetto. In 1850 it acquired the name Josefov (Joseph's Town, see pp76–85) in honour of the Emperor Joseph II whose Edict of Tolerance in 1781 lifted many restrictions on Jews. (Follow green numbers on map on p131 for route.)

Allow about 1 hour.

Take tram 17 to the Právnická Fakulta stop near Čechův most. Walk down Pařížská and bear right into Maiselova.

1 U Starého hřbitova

Tickets can be purchased for all the sights of Josefov in the Klausová synagoga (Klaus Synagogue) to your left at the end of the street. The synagogue has a print display with items dating back to 1512, the year when the first Jewish books to be printed anywhere were produced on this site. On the right is the Obřadní síň (Ceremonial Hall) which features pictures by children in the Terezín concentration camp.

Enter Starý židovský hřbitov (Old Jewish Cemetery) by the adjacent gate.

2 Starý židovský hřbitov (Old Jewish Cemetery)

In Hebrew, the name for this tranquil yet haunting place translates as 'The House of Life'; for over three centuries it was the only permitted burial place of the Prague Jews, so that some 12 layers of mortal remains had to be piled on top of one another (*see pp78–9*). The most visited tomb is that of the famous scholar Rabbi Löw. Leaving the cemetery on the south side, you pass the Pinkasova synagóga (Pinkas Synagogue). Inside is a memorial to the Czech and Slovak victims of the Holocaust. There are 77,297 names inscribed on a memorial wall, all culled from the Nazis' pedantically precise transport files.

Turn left along Široká and second right back into Maiselova.

The gateway to the Old-New Synagogue is decorated with a Star of David

3 Maiselova synagoga (Maisel Synagogue)

On your left you soon come to the Maisel Synagogue, named after the ghetto's most famous mayor, who was also Rudolf II's minister of finance. Inside is a display of ritualistic objects, such as circumcision instruments, and combs used in preparing the dead for burial.

Retrace your steps along Maiselova as far as the junction, on your right, with Červená.

4 Židovská radnice (Jewish Town Hall)

On your right is the diminutive rococo Židovská radnice (Jewish Town Hall). The cream-and-pink building's most notable feature is a Jewish clock on the front with a Hebrew dial, the hands of which move anticlockwise (Hebrew script also goes from right to left). The Town Hall is the centre of the Jewish community and incorporates a kosher restaurant.

Directly opposite is the Staronová synagoga (Old-New Synagogue), one of the earliest in Europe, with stepped brick gables and a fine-vaulted Gothic ceiling inside. A wrought-iron surround in the centre encloses the *bimah*, the lectern for readings from the Torah. For men and boys, paper skullcaps must be purchased in the vestibule before entering the sacred area.

Adjoining the Town Hall is the Vysoká synagoga (High Synagogue), which the tiny Jewish community keeps

The rococo elegance of the Jewish Town Hall

for religious services. It is usually closed to the public. The abundance of Jewish mementoes and official buildings in Josefov is due to Hitler's decision to turn this area into an official Nazi display, described as 'An Exotic Museum of an Extinct Race'.

At the end of Červená, turn right into Pařížská, and left into Široká, going as far as Vězeňská.

5 Španělská synagoga (Spanish Synagogue)

The Spanish Synagogue on Vězeňská lives up to its name, with its Moorish appearance and Alhambra-like interior. The original synagogue here was founded by Sephardic Jews fleeing the Inquisition.

Return to Pařížská and Čechův most via Dušní and Bílkova.

Kafka and Prague

Ignored in the author's lifetime, burned by the Nazis and suppressed by the Communists, the works of Franz Kafka (1883–1924) are at last being celebrated in the city of his birth.

Prague, the city that Franz Werfel claimed 'has no reality', looms over

Kafka's grave in the Jewish Cemetery

Kafka's stories as it did over his life. Praský hrad inspired *The Castle*, and the Hladová zed (Hunger Wall – *see pp71 & 123*) on Petřín Hill is thought to be the inspiration behind his story *The Great Wall of China*. Echoes of the Prague ghetto reverberate through the fantastical world of his imagination. The bumbling bureaucracy of the Habsburg administration in the 19th century supplied Kafka with numerous ideas. In retrospect, his vision seems to be a premonition of what life for the people of Prague would be like under Nazism and Stalinism, but Kafka did not live long enough to experience it.

Devotees of Kafka's work can follow his trail through Prague – to his one-time workplace (Na Poříčí 7), to the house he rented in Golden Lane on Castle Hill (No 22) and finally to his grave in the Jewish Cemetery at Strašnice (Metro line A to Želivského). The city's beauty is all around us, but reading Kafka makes us aware of another, more menacing, presence behind the beautiful façade. Kafka had this in mind, perhaps, when he wrote in his diaries: 'Prague is a dear mother with sharp claws: she never lets go of you.'

Memorial to Franz Kafka

prayers, even money – evidently the old cabbalist still exerts a spell. The headstones are works of art, with carved symbols indicating the deceased's profession, or the family name. It is a strange and haunting place, evoking both the dignity and resilience of the Jewish community.
Široka.

Vysoká synagoga (High Synagogue)

The fine Renaissance interior includes an upstairs, or 'high' prayer hall.
Červená 1. Closed to the public.

Židovská radnice (Jewish Town Hall)

The rococo aspect of the Jewish Town Hall is the result of alterations by Josef Schlesinger in 1765, when it also acquired its backwards-reading Hebraic clock. The hall is still the community centre for Prague's 2,000 Jews, and also boasts a kosher restaurant.

The Nazis employed Jewish scholars here to collect material for the planned 'Exotic Museum of an Extinct Race' (*see p76*) until early 1945, when the last of them were despatched to the camps.
Maiselova 18.

BEYOND JOSEFOV
U Hybernů (Hibernian House)

The name of this building recalls the Irish Franciscans who occupied a Baroque monastery and church at this site from 1629 until the dissolution of their establishment under Joseph II in 1786. After briefly being used as a theatre, the former church was reconstructed in neoclassical (or 'Empire') style in 1811 to plans by Johann Fischer. The imperial government used it as the Central Customs Office for Prague (hence the imperial double-headed eagle in the side-wall tympanum). After World War II it became an exhibition hall. In late 2006 the newly renovated building reopened as a theatre, staging a long-running musical called *Golem*.
Náměstí Republiky 3.
www.golem-muzikal.cz.
Metro: Náměstí Republiky.

Karolinum (Carolinum/Charles University)

Charles IV founded Europe's 35th university in Prague on 7 April 1348. The Charles University, or Karolinum, was the first such foundation in Central Europe, and its professors and students were entitled to teach and study at any other school sanctioned by the Catholic Church.

This all came into question from 1409 onwards, after the Hussite faction in Prague pressured Wenceslas IV into issuing the Decree of Kutná Hora, whereby the Czechs gained the upper hand in the university administration. There was a mass exodus of non-Bohemians (leading to the founding of Leipzig University), and Jan Hus became rector of a school increasingly

Charles University

regarded elsewhere in Europe as a nest of heretics. Eventually, in 1412, the Catholic interest rallied its forces and succeeded in having Hus ejected.

After the Battle of the White Mountain in 1620, the Jesuits (who had had their own 'Clementinum' since the mid-16th century) were allowed to annex the Carolinum.

The buildings

Some remains of the original buildings have either been laid bare during modern restoration work or were 're-Gothicised' by Joseph Mocker in the late 19th century. The finest surviving feature is the oriel window (c.1370) overlooking Ovocný trh (the fruit market). Much of the rest was reworked in Baroque style in the 18th century.

The 17th-century Assembly Hall on the first floor, with a tapestry depicting Charles IV and paintings on the organ loft by V Sychra, is unfortunately not always accessible. However, you can visit the much-restored Gothic vaults at ground-floor level, now used for exhibitions of contemporary Czech art. In the Grand Courtyard there is a modern statue of Hus by Karel Lidický.

The Carolinum is now the University Rectorate, which has faculties dispersed elsewhere around Prague. Graduation ceremonies take place at Ovocný trh 5.
Železná 9, Staré Město pedestrian zone. Tel: 224 491 250. www.cuni.cz. Cloister and halls open during exhibitions. Metro: Můstek or Náměstí Republiky.

Karlův most

Charles Bridge

In high summer, visitors jam the Charles Bridge; neo-hippies and their dogs relax; pretty girls sell knick-knacks; and often a Dixieland jazz band will supply free entertainment. In winter, the freezing mist that rises from the Vltava envelops the bridge. No other place in the city is more atmospheric, or has richer historical associations.

Of all Charles IV's ambitious undertakings, which included the building of St Vitus Cathedral, and the founding of the university and Nové Město, this 516m (1,693ft) long sandstone bridge with its 16 graceful arches captures the imagination most. He laid the foundation stone on 9 July 1357, but did not live to see the great work completed in 1383. That pleasure was reserved for his son Wenceslas IV (who murdered his Vicar-General, John Nepomuk, by having him thrown off the bridge).

Over the years the Charles Bridge has witnessed many dramatic events. During the Middle Ages, dishonest traders were suspended from the bridge in wicker baskets. In 1621 the heads of the executed Bohemian nobles who had fought against the Habsburgs were exhibited on the tower at the Staré Město end. The bridge served as the venue for the signing of the treaty that put an end to the Thirty Years War.

Architecture and statuary

The Stone Bridge (it only became the 'Charles Bridge' in 1870) replaced an earlier Romanesque one named after Judith of Thuringia, wife of Vladislav I. It is not quite straight, having been built using the Judith Bridge's land foundations on each side of the river, but with midstream piers placed slightly to the south of the previous construction.

The bridge towers

All that is left from the Romanesque period are some piers sunk in the river bed, and the smaller of the two bridge towers at the Malá Strana end, the latter having been rebuilt during the Renaissance era.

It is joined to a higher tower built by King George of Poděbrady, which is largely an imitation of the tower on the opposite bank. At the Staré Město end is the impressive Gothic tower designed by Petr Parléř. St Vitus is portrayed on the east façade, flanked by Charles IV (on the left) and Wenceslas IV (on the right). Above them are St Adalbert and St Sigismund, patron saints of Bohemia, and below them the coats of arms of the Czech Crown Lands, together with a veiled kingfisher, the heraldic symbol of Wenceslas IV.

The statues

A remarkable feature of the Charles Bridge is the Baroque sculptures of saints, erected between 1683 and 1714 on each side. Originally, there had been only one stark crucifixion scene on the bridge, but in the late 17th century Bernini's sumptuous statuary for the Ponte dei Angeli in Rome inspired a similar plan for Prague.

The Jesuits, keen to promote the cult of St John Nepomuk, put up his statue by Jan Brokoff (in the middle of the north side) in 1683. The Brokoff dynasty (Jan, Jan Michael and Ferdinand Maximilian) supplied a number of fine works.

Some of the older statues have been replaced with copies; several uninspired neo-Gothic works went up in the 19th century. The finest Baroque sculpture is Matthias Braun's representation of St Luitgarde and the Crucifixion (1710) on the south side, the fourth from the Malá Strana bank. A modern work of some distinction is Karel Dvořák's Sts Cyril and Methodius (1938) on the north side, the fifth statue from the Staré Město bank.

Trams: 12, 17, 18, 20, 22 or 23. Metro: Staroměstská or Malostranská.

Karlův most

A new day dawns on the Charles Bridge

Plaque to Joseph II on the wall of the Clementinum

Klementinum (Clementinum)

In 1556, Ferdinand I summoned 40 Jesuit monks to Prague. They took over the Dominicans' church of St Clement and founded the Clementinum, a centre of learning and propaganda for the faith. It continued to expand up to the mid-18th century, swallowing up 32 houses, three churches, several gardens and even the heretical Carolinum (*see p84*). After the disbanding of the Jesuits, the now non-heretical Charles University moved its library to the Clementinum. It currently houses the National Library of the Czech Republic, and the State Technical Library, with an estimated 5 million volumes, numerous incunabula and manuscripts. Its most celebrated item is the *Codex Vyšegradensis* of 1085.

The architects chiefly involved in building the Clementinum were Carlo Lurago, Francesco Caratti and (later) František Kaňka.

Kostel svatého Klimenta (St Clement's Church)

This is the Prague base of the Uniate Church (halfway between Orthodoxy and Catholicism). Entry is difficult, but it is worth trying in order to see the frescoes by Jan Hiebel depicting the life of St Clement, and the fine sandstone sculptures of the Church fathers and the four Evangelists by Matthias Braun. *Open: times vary. Apply at the sacristy if closed.*

Vlašská kaple (The Italian Chapel)

Built in 1597 for the community of Italian painters, sculptors and masons in Prague, the chapel has an elliptical form inspired by the Roman Baroque. It still belongs to the Italian state. *Located between St Clement's and the east end of the Church of the Holy Saviour on Karlova. Entry is difficult.*

Zrcadlová kaple (The Marian Chapel)

František Kaňka completed this chapel in 1730. The name Zrcadlová kaple ('Chapel of Mirrors') is a reference to the mirrors in the ceiling. It served as the private chapel of the Brotherhood of Our Lady; hence Hiebel's ceiling fresco depicting the life of the Virgin. Concerts and exhibitions are regularly held here.

The halls

Kaňka and Hiebel designed and decorated the **Jesuit Library** or 'Baroque Hall' in the east wing, with its Salomonic columns and ceiling fresco of *The Temple of Wisdom*. Also frescoed by Hiebel, the **Mathematical Hall** contains a collection of table clocks.

The **Mozart Room** is a full-blown example of rococo, with beautiful paintings and finely carved bookcases. *Access to the Clementinum is from Karlova or Křížovnická ulice. Tel: 221 663 111; www.nkp.cz*
Metro: Staroměstská. Trams: 17 & 18 to Staroměstská.

Kostel svatého Františka Serafinského
(Church of St Francis Seraphicus)

This was the knights' own church (*see p39 and below*). On the street corner is Jan Bendl's statue of St Wenceslas.

Kostel svatého Salvátora
(Church of the Holy Saviour)

This Jesuit church on the east side of the square forms part of the Clementinum. It took over a century (1593–1714) to complete. The rich (now blackened and crumbling) statuary on the façade is by Jan Bendl. Carlo Lurago was the main architect, while the lavish stucco inside is the work of Domenico Galli. Karel

Stádník's modern (1985) glass and metal altar symbolising the cosmos is in harmony with the interior.
Trams: 17 & 18 to Staroměstská.

Křižovnické náměstí
(Knights of the Cross Square)

The coronation route of the Bohemian kings passed along Karlova and across the Knights of the Cross Square on to the Charles Bridge, before winding its way through the Lesser Quarter up to the Hrad. The square is named after the hospice Order of the Knights of the Cross with a Red Star (Knights of St John), who were the keepers of the Judith Bridge in the 13th century.

Next to the bridge is Ernst Hähnel's cast-iron statue of Charles IV. The outbreak of the 1848 revolution in Prague prevented its planned inauguration, which was due to be on the 500th anniversary of the founding of Charles University.

The Church of the Holy Saviour's façade is decorated with statues of angels and saints

Karlův most

Walk: Národní třída to Křížovnické náměstí

This route encompasses places associated with a vanishing Habsburg empire, an aspiring playwright, aggressive agitators and astute propagandists.

Allow 1½ hours.

Begin at Národní divadlo (National Theatre), reached by trams 6, 9, 17, 18, 21, 22 & 23.

1 Národní divadlo (National Theatre)

The neo-Renaissance National Theatre opened in 1881 with a performance of Smetana's patriotic opera *Libuše*. It is lavishly decorated inside with allegorical and historical themes by leading artists of the day. Opposite it,

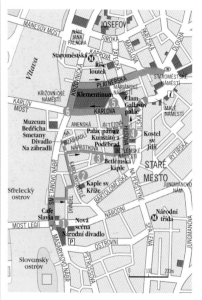

on the corner of Národní and the embankment, is the Café Slavia. In the interwar years this was the haunt of literati, including Nobel Laureate Jaroslav Seifert; under the Husák regime, opposition writers met here to pass around their *samizdat* manuscripts.

A few steps north on the embankment brings you to the monument to the Habsburg emperor Franz I.

Cross the square into Karolíny Světlé.

2 Kaple svatého Kříže (Chapel of the Holy Cross)

On the right is the Romanesque Kaple svatého Kříže, Chapel of the Holy Cross (*see p56*).

A detour north brings you towards Anenské náměstí and the Divadlo Na zábradlí, the theatre where Václav Havel began his underground career in the 1960s as a stagehand. Turn right up Náprstkova, which brings you to Betlémské náměstí.

3 Betlémské náměstí (Bethlehem Square)

The square takes its name from the gabled Betlémská kaple (Bethlehem Chapel) (*see p38*), built by pre-Hussite reformists who had been denied the right to build a church, which is why a 'chapel' could accommodate 3,000! The Communists encouraged the building of the present replica: Hussites were regarded as ideologically sound.

Turn left into Husova.

4 Husova

Shortly on the right is **Kostel svatého Jiljí** (**St Giles's Church**). A touching fresco inside shows the hermit stricken by an arrow fired by an archer of the Visigoth king. The arrow had been destined for St Giles's pet deer, which looks surprised but unharmed.

A detour to your left along Řetězová takes you to Palác pánů z Kunštátu a Poděbrad (Palace of the Lords of Kunštát and Poděbrady – No 3) which has a perfectly preserved Romanesque cellar (*see p115*).

Retrace your steps. Continue along Husova to the junction with Karlova. A detour right can be made here to the picturesque Malé náměstí; otherwise turn left. Note the imposing Clam-Gallas Palace (see p113) beyond the junction. Palace open: May–Sept Tue–Sun 10am–6pm. Admission charge.

5 Karlova

Shortly on the right is the Klementinum (Clementinum) (*see*

p88). It was a centre of learning, as well as propaganda, and Johannes Kepler once scanned the night skies from its observatory.

Karlova opens into Křížovnické náměstí.

6 Křížovnické náměstí (Knights of the Cross Square)

This square (*see p89*) has two churches – a Jesuit one and the Franciscan Church of St Francis Seraphicus (*see p39*) that belonged to the Knights of St John, guardians of the Judith Bridge (Charles Bridge's predecessor). By the bridge is a cast-iron statue of Charles IV.

From Křížovnické náměstí you can either stroll straight on to Malá Strana across the Karlův most (Charles Bridge) or turn right and right again to follow Platnéřská to Mariánské náměstí.

Statue of Charles IV overlooking the bridge that bears his name

Malá Strana

Malá Strana, the 'Lesser Quarter', is at once intimate and grandiose. Crowded with sumptuous Baroque palaces and churches, its narrow cobbled streets tail off into green garden-oases of silence, or snake towards the river through irregular medieval squares.

In 1257, the ambitious Přemysl Otakar II founded a 'New Town' in an area on the west bank of the Vltava hitherto consisting only of scattered communities. The latter included the Knights of St John, whose headquarters were at the end of the Judith Bridge, as well as a few market traders and the Jews of Újezd. The knights were allowed to stay, while the Jews and the other inhabitants were summarily evicted to make way for German merchants. New towns, directly dependent on royal privilege, were vital for the king's exchequer, and represented Otakar's attempt to outmanoeuvre the Czech nobility, the latter having won the right to set their own level of taxation.

Otakar's 'New Town' was given the name 'Lesser Quarter' under Charles IV, who founded his own 'Nové Město' on the opposite bank of the river. The area was widely damaged in 1419 by the Hussites, and further devastated by the great fire of 1541. From the ashes rose Renaissance houses, together with a large Italian quarter that was established by the hundreds of Italian artisans attracted to Prague during the construction boom under Ferdinand and Rudolf (names like Vlašská (Italian) Street recall their presence).

THE WORLD OF JAN NERUDA

Nerudova, the street in Malá Strana named after the celebrated Czech writer and journalist Jan Neruda (1834–91), rises sharply from Malostranské náměstí towards the Hrad. Near its summit, at No 47, is the house where Neruda was born, and the streets round about are the settings for his *Tales of the Lesser Quarter* (1878). No other writer evokes the day-to-day life of 19th-century Prague. Each story is a sharp vignette of late-Habsburg Prague.

Neruda, the son of a charwoman and a tobacconist, was in many ways typical of the milieu he describes. He fell foul of the conservative Czech nationalists, while his adherence to the 'Young Czech' cause made him suspect in the eyes of German officialdom. Deserted by friends and derided by his enemies, he died unjustly discredited and neglected.

Malá Strana acquired its present importance when Catholic nobles loyal to the Habsburgs were granted most of it in the 1620s, and built their fabulous palaces. The diminutive Baroque town – it encompasses a mere 60 hectares (148 acres) – has survived the turmoil of recent history almost unscathed. The main scenes of Miloš Forman's film *Amadeus* were set in virtually the same town as that which was visited by Mozart in 1787, when he stayed with his patron Count Thun in what is now the British Embassy.

The Lesser Quarter's last great social upheaval was in 1948 when the Communists solved the housing shortage by dividing its palaces into apartments. Thereafter, the world's potentially most glamorous council houses slowly decayed for 40 years. After the restitution law of 1990,

Nerudova, where every door tells a tale

many have been taken over by private concerns and have been exquisitely renovated.

Malá Strana. Trams: 12, 20, 22 & 23 to Malostranské náměstí. Metro: Malostranská.

Malá Strana – a bird's-eye view

Malá Strana

Walk: Malá Strana

This walk covers many of the most interesting sights of the Malá Strana (Lesser Quarter). The nobles built their great palaces here to be close to (or, in Wallenstein's case, to rival) the Royal Court of Hradčany.

Allow 2 hours.

Begin at the Malostranská metro station (also the tram stop for Nos 12, 18, 20, 22 & 23) and turn left into Valdštejnská.

1 Valdštejnská

The street is filled with the palatial residences of the German nobility imported by the Habsburgs. The Valdštejnsky palác (Wallenstein Palace)

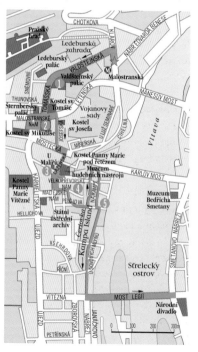

occupies the entire east side of Valdštejnské náměstí at the end of the street. Albrecht von Waldstein ('Wallenstein' in English) was the greatest imperial commander in the Thirty Years War. His vaulting ambition proved his downfall: Emperor Ferdinand had him assassinated when he set his sights on becoming king of Bohemia. *Continue into Tomášská and Malostranské náměstí (see pp96–7).*

2 Malostranské náměstí

The whole of the west side of Malostranské náměstí (Lesser Quarter Square) is occupied by the Lichtenštejnský palác (Liechtenstein Palace), home of the Liechtenstein who condemned the Protestant leaders to death in 1621, while in the Smiřický Palace to the north the plot was hatched that led to the defenestration of Ferdinand's Catholic councillors in 1618. Lording over these webs of intrigue is the Baroque Kostel svatého Mikuláše (St Nicholas Church – *see p97*), the greatest masterwork in Prague of the Dientzenhofers, father and son. *Walk east along Letenská, turning immediately right into Josefská, and passing the Kostel svatého Josefa (St Joseph's Church). Turn left into Mostecká and then right into Lázeňská.*

3 Lázeňská

A few minutes on foot brings you to the area associated with the Maltese Knights (of the Order of St John), as recalled in the names of its two diminutive and picturesque squares: Maltézské náměstí (Maltese Square), and Velkopřevorské náměstí (Grand

Prior's Square). A relic of their function as keepers of the first bridge across the Vltava is the chain hung above the high altar of their church, Kostel Panny Marie pod řetězem (Church of Our Lady below the Chain, accessible for Sunday Mass at 10.30am, held in French). At No 11 Maltese Square is the elegant little U Malířů (Painters' Tavern), now an expensive restaurant. *Continue to the adjoining Velkopřevorské náměstí (Grand Prior's Square).*

4 Velkopřevorské náměstí

The Palace of the Grand Prior used to host the Muzeum hudebních nastrojů (Musical Instruments Museum). A back wall has become an unofficial shrine to John Lennon, with graffiti portraits making him look like a Byzantine saint. *Return to Maltézské náměstí and enter Nosticova. Turn left on Pelclova and cross the bridge to Kampa Island.*

5 Kampa Island

The bridge spans the Čertovka, or Devil's Stream, named after the tricky sprite thought to inhabit it (or possibly just an abusive reference to a famously grumpy local washerwoman).

It is worth taking a turn round the delightful 'island' and perhaps stopping for a drink at one of the pavement cafés below Charles Bridge on Na Kampe. *Leave Kampa by the southern end and climb up on to most Legií (the Bridge of the Legions). On the far side are the Národní divadlo (National Theatre) and tram stops.*

The serene beauty of the streets on Kampa Island as seen from the Charles Bridge

Malostranské náměstí

Once the outer bailey of Prague Castle, the Lesser Quarter Square became the focus of the small town founded by Otakar II in 1257. In the Middle Ages a Romanesque rotunda dedicated to St Wenceslas stood in the middle of it, along with a pillory and a gallows. The Town Hall was established in the 15th century and later a parish church of St Nicholas (Kostel svatého Mikuláše) was built, dividing the upper and lower halves of the square.

The Lower Square

Gothic, Renaissance and Baroque elements mingle gracefully in the lower part of the square. To the west it is closed by the rear walls of St Nicholas and the former Jesuit College. In front of these is the rococo Grömling Palace (built by Josef Jäger in 1773); the Radetzky Café (named after the Austrian general who put down the Italian rebellion against the Habsburgs in 1848) was opened on the ground floor, and became a haunt of the Prague literati, including Kafka, Brod and Werfel. The name 'Radetzky' did not survive the rise of Czech nationalism – its latest incarnation is as a trendy tapas restaurant named Square.

On the east side of the square, at No 21, is the former Town Hall (Malostranská radnice). It was here that Protestant groups hammered out the Bohemian Confession of 1575 that guaranteed the freedom of religion.

On the north side of the Lower Square are the Sternberg Palace (No 15), where the great fire of 1541 broke out, and the Smiřický Palace (No 18), where the dissident Czech nobles plotted the overthrow of Ferdinand II's hated Catholic councillors on 22 May 1618. On the following day, they matched words by deeds by throwing the councillors out of the windows of the Bohemian Chancellery (the third Prague defenestration).

The Upper Square

At the centre of the square is Giovanni Alliprandi's Plague Column (1715). The whole of the west side is occupied by the Liechtenstein Palace, whose neoclassical façade dates to 1791. The Liechtensteins lost their Czech possessions (about ten times the size of the present Grand Duchy) in 1918; the restitution law passed after the Velvet Revolution only covered what had been grabbed by the state after 1948, or they could have received large chunks of the Czech Republic.

Kostel svatého Mikuláše (St Nicholas Church)

This beautiful basilica, opposite the Liechtenstein Palace, is regarded by many as the finest church in Prague, if not in Central Europe. Christoph Dientzenhofer, commissioned by the Jesuits, built the elegant façade (1710) and also completed the nave, the side-chapels and the galleries before his death in 1722. His son Kilián Ignác built the choir and the ambitious dome (1752); the townspeople refused to enter the church until a commission of experts had pronounced it safe.

An outstanding feature of the interior is Lukáš Kracker's 1,500sq m (16,145sq ft) illusionist fresco on the ceiling of the nave, showing the Apotheosis of St Nicholas. The outsized statues of the early fathers of the Church under the cupola are by Ignaz Platzer, who also sculpted that of St Nicholas above the high altar. The superb rococo pulpit (1765) by Richard and Peter Práchner is decorated with allegories of Faith, Hope and Charity; rather oddly juxtaposed is a scene of John the Baptist being beheaded. The splendour of the basilica makes a visit one of the most moving experiences.

Tel: 257 534 215. Open: 9am–5pm. Admission charge. Trams: 12, 20, 22 & 23 to Malostranské náměstí. Metro: Malostranská.

Malostranské náměstí

High Baroque sculpture inside the Basilica of St Nicholas

Museums

Although Prague has a clutch of museums covering natural history, art and geology, its best are the peculiar but elegant Mucha Museum, the Museum of Flight and the Museum of Toys.

Armádní muzeum (Army Museum)

Formerly the Museum of the Resistance and the Czechoslovak Army, this has now been revamped to make it more informative than its predecessor. Topics covered include the story of the Czech Legions in World War I and the assassination of the Nazi 'Reichs-protektor' Reinhard Heydrich during World War II (*see pp42 & 142*).
U Památníku 2, Žižkov. Tel: 973 204 924. Open: Tue–Sun 10am–6pm. Admission charge.
Buses: 133 & 207 to U Památníku. Metro: Florenc.

Expozice Franze Kafky (Franz Kafka Permanent Exhibition)

Kafka's life and works are shown in words and pictures.
U Radnice 5, just off Staroměstské náměstí. Open: Tue–Fri 10am–6pm, Sat 10am–5pm. Tram & metro: Staroměstská. The bookshop is well worth a visit.

Letecké muzeum Kbely (Museum of Flight)

Some 80 of the 200 aeroplanes in this museum are on display. The capsule in which the first Czech cosmonaut landed back on earth (1978) may also be seen, and there is extensive information on the former Czechoslovakia's participation in space research.
Kbely airport (Praha 9). Open: 1 May–31 Oct Tue–Sun 10am–6pm. Admission charge. Metro: B to Českomoravská, then buses 259 & 280 to Letecké Muzeum.

Lobkovický palác národní historické muzeum (Lobkowicz Palace National History Museum)

A visit to this museum is best combined with a tour of Castle Hill (*see p54*). Exhibits include St Wenceslas's sword and material relating to the Hussite wars and the Battle of the White Mountain.
Jiřská 3, Hradčany. Open: daily 10.30am–6pm. Admission charge.

Trams: 22 or 23 to Pražský hrad.
Metro: Malostranská.

Muchovo muzeum
(Mucha Museum)

A superb exhibition of the works of the graphic artist and designer Alphonse Mucha. The museum also has a good gift shop with some fine Mucha posters.
Panská 7, Nové město. www.mucha.cz.
Open: daily 10am–6pm. Free admission.
Metro: Muzeum or Můstek.

Muzeum hlavního města Prahy
(Museum of the City of Prague)

This museum contains substantial archaeological finds, plus impressive statuary and sculpture, ranging from a Gothic Madonna of 1383 to a fine bronze of Hercules by Adrian de Vries. The Baroque wood sculptures are by the finest Bohemian masters, including Jan Bendl, Matthias Braun and Ferdinand Brokoff.

A curiosity is Antonín Langweil's model of historic Prague, which took him eight years to make (1826–34). Some 2,228 buildings have been lovingly recreated, giving a unique scale picture of the city in the early 19th century.
Na Poříčí 52. www.muzeumprahy.cz.
Open: Tue–Sun 9am–6pm. Admission charge. First Thur in every month is a symbolic 1kč (open 9am–8pm).
Trams: 8 & 24 to Florenc.

The exceptional art of Alphonse Mucha is on display at the Mucha Museum

Museums

Muzeum hraček (Toy Museum)

The second-largest collection of toys in the world, in the beautiful Supreme Burgrave's house, it includes ancient as well as modern toys and games.
Jiřská, Prague Castle. Open: daily 9am–5.30pm.
Trams: 12, 18, 22 & 23.

Muzeum komunismu (Museum of Communism)

Wedged between a McDonald's and a casino is a museum that portrays the dreams, reality and nightmare of the post-war Communist regime.
Na Příkopě 10. Tel: 224 212 966. www.muzeumkomunismu.cz. Open: daily 9am–9pm. Admission charge. Metro: Můstek.

Muzeum městské hromadné dopravy (City Transport Museum)

Houses a collection of historic vehicles, from 1886 to the present day.
Patočkova 4, Praha 6. Tel: 296 124 900. Open: Apr–Nov Sat, Sun & holidays 9am–5pm; by appointment in winter (Dec–Mar). Metro: Hradčanská, then trams 1, 2, 15, 18 & 25 to Vozovna střešovice.

Muzeum policie (Police Museum)

Covers the history of the Czech (and Czechoslovak) police forces. There are also some interesting displays on criminology and specific crimes, weapons, forensic sources and the like.

Ke Karlovu 1, Praha 2. Tel: 224 922 183. Open: Tue–Sun 10am–5pm. Admission charge. Metro: I P Pavlova.

Náprstkovo muzeum (Náprstek Museum)

The museum contains artefacts from Native American, Oceanian, African and Asian cultures.
Betlémské náměstí 1, Praha 1. Tel: 224 497 500. Open: Tue–Sun 9am–noon, 12.45–5.30pm. Admission charge. Every first Fri in the month is free. Trams: 6, 9, 18, 21, 22 & 23 to Národní divadlo. Metro: Národní třída.

Národní muzeum (National Museum)

The original project for the National Museum united the aspirations of the Czech and German populations, but by the time the present heavy neo-Renaissance building (the museum's third home) was completed in 1891, it had become a pugnaciously Czech affair. Inside are somewhat forbidding departments of zoology and botany, archaeology, palaeontology and mineralogy to wade through.

The focus of the building is the heroic marble Pantheon. It is a huge, richly decorated space under the cupola, with sculptures of famous Czechs, and lunettes painted by Václav Brožík and František Ženíšek showing major events from the nation's past. Six over-lifesize statues stand next to the pillars: four giants of Bohemia's

The harsh reality of the post-war Communist years is laid bare at the Museum of Communism

past – Jan Hus, Jan Comenius, František Palacký and Tomáš Masaryk – plus two relative lightweights – Count Šternberk, the museum's founder, and the writer Jan Neruda.

Václavské náměstí 68.
Tel: 224 497 111. www.nm.cz.
Open: daily 10am–6pm (5pm Oct–Apr).
Closed every first Tue in the month.
Admission charge (free admission every first Mon in the month).
Metro: Muzeum.

Národní technicke muzeum (National Technical Museum)

A marvellous display of historic transport, from imperial railway carriages to early sports cars. Space is also devoted to photography, astronomy, mining and much else. Currently closed for renovation. Set to reopen by 2010.
Kostelní 42, Letná, Praha 7.
Tel: 233 374 641. www.ntm.cz.

TOMÁŠ GARRIGUE MASARYK

Czechoslovakia, in its short existence (1918–92), produced two statesmen who won the respect of the world: Václav Havel and Tomáš Masaryk (1850–1937). Masaryk was of humble origin – an illegitimate child brought up by Slovak peasants. He rose to become a professor of philosophy and a Social Democratic MP in the Reichsrat (Parliament) of the Austro-Hungarian Empire. In exile during World War I, he laid the foundation of the new Czechoslovak Republic, which proved to be a model of stability and democracy under his presidency (1918–35), although emphatically a pan-Slavic nation rather than a more multicultural one.

Call for opening hours and admission charges. Trams: 1, 8, 15, 25 & 26 to Letenské náměstí.

Poštovní muzeum (Postal Museum)

This rather charming and little-frequented museum has a stamp collection on the ground floor and some homely prints upstairs demonstrating that a postman's lot is not necessarily a happy one. It covers Czechoslovak and European stamps, as well as stamps of the Czech Republic.
Vávrův dům, Nové mlýny 2. Tel: 222 312 006. www.cpost.cz. Open: Tue–Sun 9am–5pm. Admission charge. Trams: 5, 8 & 14 to Dlouhá Třída.

Uměleckoprůmyslové muzeum (Museum of Decorative Arts)

Only a tiny proportion of this museum's vast hoard of Renaissance to 19th-century treasures is on permanent display. A great deal of that is furniture, including some fine escritoires, cabinets and clocks. The main focus is on 16th- to 19th-century European and Czech handicrafts, including ceramics, textiles, glass, fashion items and metalwork. A selection of applied art is also on show at the Tyršovo Museum.
Ulice 17, Listopadu 2. Tel: 251 093 111. www.upm.cz. Open: Tue–Sun 10am–6pm. Admission charge. Trams: 17 & 18. Metro: Staroměstská.

The façade of the National Museum

Laterna Magika

'What is life? An illusion, a shadow, a story . . .' wrote the 17th-century Spanish dramatist Calderón, a reflection which might well be applied to Prague's avant-garde illusionist theatres.

The cunning use of spectacle, illusion and music has its roots at least as far back as the propagandist art and drama sponsored by the Jesuits in the Baroque age. Modern technology opened the way to a new form of multimedia spectacle first developed by Alfréd Redok in the 1950s. His

Laterna Magika (Magic Lantern) shows made sophisticated use of lighting and film projection, and won world acclaim at the Brussels Expo of 1958. The idea has proved a runaway success at the box office. Its more or less imitative spin-offs include Theatrum Novum and the Laterna Animata.

The show is a mix of live acting and scenic *coups de théâtre* brought about by film or slide projection and dramatic lighting effects. The third ingredient is music. Particularly successful are reworked myths, such as that of the *Odyssey* in terms of 'the common dawn and early childhood of today's Europe'.

It has to be admitted that there are times when gimmickry overwhelms the drama. On the other hand, the criticism that Laterna Magika is merely a faked theatrical 'happening' put on for visitors misses the point. The shows are popular because they are exciting and brilliantly staged. These performances are a unique part of Prague's theatre culture.

Productions in the repertoire include *Magic Circus*, *The Minotaur*, *Odysseus* and *Carmina Burana*. The shows take place in the Nová Scéna of the National Theatre. For booking arrangements, see pp152–3.

The Magic Lantern is an experience unique to Prague

MUSIC MUSEUMS
Bertramka

This charming 17th-century villa (and gardens), which houses the memorial to Wolfgang Mozart and Mr & Mrs Dušek, is named after its second owner, František Bertram. However, it owes its fame to the fact that Mozart stayed here with his friends Josefa Dušková, the opera singer, and her composer husband, František Dušek. Mozart was allegedly locked in one of the rooms until he had completed a long-promised aria for Josefa; he may also have completed the overture to *Don Giovanni* here.

There is an exhibition of the composer's life and work in the villa, and a bust of him by Tomáš Seidan in the garden. Charming concerts of

Statue of Bedřich Smetana

MOZART IN PRAGUE

Mozart arrived for his second visit to Prague in the autumn of 1787 with a new opera under his arm. *The Seraglio* and *The Marriage of Figaro* had already brought him fame with the musically sophisticated Prague public; *Don Giovanni*, premiered on 29 October at the Estates Theatre (*see p132*), was an even greater triumph. *La Clemenza di Tito*, premiered in the autumn of 1791, was considered old-fashioned and was not well received. Mozart died two months later on 5 December in Vienna, virtually unmourned by his compatriots. However, Prague staged a grand memorial service for him on 14 December in the Kostel svatého Mikuláše (St Nicholas Church) of the Lesser Quarter. The church, with a capacity of 4,000 people, was filled to overflowing and carriages blocked the surrounding streets. Josefa Dušková led the requiem singers.

Mozart arias and other works are held in the villa and in the gardens in the summer months.

Mozartova 169, Smíchov. Tel: 257 318 461. www.bertramka.com. Open: daily 9.30am–6pm (4pm in winter). Admission charge. Trams: 4, 6, 7 & 9 to Bertramka. Metro: (line B) to Anděl, and a 10-minute walk.

Muzeum Antonína Dvořáka (Antonín Dvořák Museum – Vila Amerika)

The name of this gem of a Baroque villa, built by Kilián Ignác Dientzenhofer, and with statues from Matthias Braun's workshop, refers to a hotel that used to stand nearby, not to Dvořák's famous *New World Symphony*.

The Dvořák collection includes musical scores and correspondence. One of the greatest of the 19th-century Romantic composers, Antonín Dvořák (1841–1904) drew much inspiration from Czech folk music.

Ke Karlovu 20. Tel: 224 918 013. Open: Tue–Sun 10am–5pm. Admission charge. Trams: 4, 6, 10, 16, 22 & 23.
Metro: I P Pavlova.

Muzeum Bedřicha Smetany (Bedřich Smetana Museum)

A modern statue of the great Czech composer sitting under a willow with his back to his beloved Vltava is almost the only item of note in this otherwise undistinguished museum on the life and works of Smetana (1824–84). Smetana composed the music most closely identified with the patriotic aspirations of Bohemia. His best-known works are *The Bartered Bride* and *Dalibor*, and his tone poem *My Country* contains a famous passage beautifully evoking the surging waters of the Vltava.

Novotného lávka 1. Tel: 222 220 082.
Open: daily 10am–5pm.
Closed: Tue. Admission charge.
Trams: 17 & 18 to Karlovy lázně.
Metro: Staroměstská.

The Dvořák Museum, housed in a Baroque villa designed by Kilián Ignác Dientzenhofer

Musical Prague

'Music', according to an old Prague saying, 'was born of necessity and became a necessity.' It was in the 17th century, however, that musical culture truly burgeoned in Bohemia and Moravia, particularly in the court of Rudolf II and under the influence of Prince-Bishop Karl Liechtenstein-Kastelcorn of Olomouc. By the 18th century, Czech composers were famous all over Europe, including Koželuh, Mysliveček, Vranický and Zelenka.

Prague audiences are traditionally more musically literate than elsewhere. As early as the 1720s, the public could buy cheap seats in private theatres, where censorship was also lax compared with the stiff court opera in Vienna. Thus, the people of Prague understood and loved the music of Mozart at a time when Vienna turned its back on him.

Nowadays, Prague's year-round music festivals, most famously the international Prague Spring Music Festival in the last two weeks of May, attract music lovers from all over the world (*see p154 for details*).

Throughout the year churches, former convents and Baroque palaces ring to the sound of sacred and

Music is central to the lives of many Czechs

In the spring Prague is a magnet for music lovers from around the world

profane harmonies. The giants of Czech music, Bedřich Smetana (1824–84), Antonín Dvořák (1841–1904) and the Moravian Leoš Janáček (1854–1938), tend to dominate the symphony programmes. Opera and symphony concerts are held in the great auditoria built during the late 19th-century boom of patriotic culture: the National Theatre (Národní divadlo, 1881, *see p90*), the Rudolfinum (1884), and the Municipal House (Obecní dům, 1911, *see pp124–5*); but many delightful works by minor composers of the Czech Baroque are played in such romantic settings as Bazilika svatého Jiří (St George's Basilica) on Castle Hill (*see p63*).

In the 18th century the English musicologist Charles Burney gave Prague the title of 'The Music Conservatory of Europe'. Were he to come back now, he would see no reason to change his opinion. Hurrying figures with cello cases are still to be seen on the streets, and on languid summer afternoons melodious strains waft from many an open window.

STÁLÉ EXPOZICE NÁRODNÍ GALERIE
(National Gallery Permanent Collections)
Anežský klášter
(St Agnes' Convent)
Medieval Art in Bohemia and Central Europe

The cloister and convent feature Czech Gothic art, and also house long-term but temporary exhibitions of Czech art and sculpture (*see pp28–9*).
U Milosrdných 17. Tel: 224 810 628. Open: Tue–Sun 10am–6pm. Admission charge. Metro: Staroměstská or Náměstí Republiky, then trams 5, 8 or 14 to Dlouhá třída.

Klášter svatého Jiří na Pražském hradě (St George's Convent at Prague Castle)
Collection of old Bohemian art

The gallery is divided into two sections: Gothic art in the basement and at ground-floor level, Baroque works on the first floor. Among the former are fine examples of International Gothic or 'Beautiful Style'. One of the earliest free-standing sculptures (1373) is the bronze *St George and the Dragon*.

High points are the nine-panelled altarpiece from the Cistercian monastery at Vyssí Brod and paintings of saints by Master Theodoric. Arresting Baroque works include Bartolomaeus Spranger's *The Risen Christ* and sculptures by Maximilian Brokoff and Matthias Braun, in particular the latter's sculpture of St Jude.

St George's Convent

Jiřské náměstí 33. Hradčany. Tel: 257 531 644. Open: Tue–Sun 10am–6pm. Admission charge. Trams: 22 or 23 to Pražský hrad. Metro: Malostranská.

Šternberský palác
(Sternberg Palace)
Old European art

Albrecht Dürer's *The Feast of the Rose Garlands* is the gallery's most celebrated possession, which also features early European art of the 14th and 15th centuries, Dutch paintings of the 15th century, Roman schools of the 17th and 18th centuries, Flemish 17th-century paintings and German and Austrian paintings of the 15th to 18th centuries. Among these are some fine works by El Greco, Holbein, Rembrandt, Rubens and Van Dyck.
Hradčanské náměstí 15. Tel: 233 090 570. Open: Tue–Sun 10am–6pm. Admission charge. Trams: 22 or 23 to Pražský hrad. Metro: Malostranská.

Veletržní palác (Palace of Fairs)

Designed for the Prague Trade Fair of 1928, this huge glass-fronted building was described by Le Corbusier, the famous 20th-century architect, as simply 'breathtaking'.

Among the many outstanding collections of 19th- and 20th-century Czech and European art are *Green Rye* (1889) by Van Gogh, *Two Women Among the Flowers* (1875) by Monet, and one of Gauguin's Tahiti paintings, *Flight* (1902). There are also works by Braque, Chagall, Derain, Dufy, Picasso and Vlaminck. Sculptures include works by Henri Laurens and Rodin. *Dukelských hrdinů 47. Tel: 224 301 111. Open: Tue–Sun 10am–6pm, Thur until 9pm. Admission charge. Trams: 12, 14, 15 & 17.*

Zámek Zbraslav (Zbraslav Chateau)

Permanent exhibition of Asian art

This former monastery where non-European works of art are housed is well worth the trek. It also holds temporary exhibitions.

Ke Krňovu 1, Zbraslav nad Vltavou, Praha V. Tel: 257 921 638. Open: Tue–Sun 10am–6pm. Admission charge. Metro: (line B) to Smíchovské nádraží, then buses 129, 241, 243 or 255 to Zbraslavské náměstí.

Sternberg Palace houses art treasures spanning six centuries

Palaces

The majority of Prague's noble palaces are today occupied by government institutions, museums or embassies. Most are the product of the building boom in Baroque times.

After the Battle of the White Mountain in 1620, German aristocrats and war profiteers loyal to the Habsburgs took over property that had belonged to the now-exiled Bohemian nobility, or bought up land at depressed prices. The most spectacular example of megalomaniac building from this period is the huge Valdštejnský palác (Wallenstein Palace) in Malá Strana (*see pp116–17*); to make way for it 23 houses, three gardens and a brickworks were demolished.

A Baroque palace was designed to display its owner's wealth and importance – the secular equivalent of Baroque church architecture with its fabulous ornamentation. This period of ostentatious display lasted until the second half of the 18th century, when centralising reforms under Maria Theresa and Joseph II reduced the power and importance of the aristocracy. Few palaces were built after about 1750, although a number of existing ones were rebuilt or refurbished to reflect contemporary taste.

The palaces listed below have been chosen for their aesthetic or historical interest. The list excludes those described in the contexts of Hradčanské náměstí (*see pp68–9*), Malostranské náměstí (*see pp96–7*), and Staroměstské náměstí (*see pp126–9*).

Černínský palác (Černín Palace)

Four generations of Černíns and as many architects worked on this enormous palace (its façade is 135m/443ft wide). Jan Černín, who conceived the project, was ambassador in Venice, where he is said to have persuaded Bernini to do the first sketch for the building. It was not completed until 1720. Since 1932 it has belonged to the Ministry of Foreign Affairs. In 1948 Jan Masaryk, the only non-Communist in the government, mysteriously 'fell' to his death from its upper floor – possibly the last Prague defenestration.

Loretánské náměstí 5, Hradčany. The palace is not open to the public. Trams: 22 or 23 to Pohořelec.

Clam-Gallasův palác (Clam-Gallas Palace)

The palace was built between 1713 and 1719 by Domenico Canevalle to a design by the great Viennese architect Johann Bernhard Fischer von Erlach. For such a noble building it may seem rather cramped in its surroundings on Husova. Indeed, the owner had assumed that he would be able to demolish the block opposite so that his palace would look on to a square. Not surprisingly, the residents had other ideas, so that a mortified Count Gallas had to be content with what he had.

Notable are the Atlas figures by the two doorways, the work of Matthias Braun, who also made the rest of the sculptural decoration. Inside there is a grand staircase with stucco by Santo Rossi, and above it a fresco (*The Triumph of Apollo*) by Carlo Carlone. The city archives are now housed in the palace, which means that you can usually wander in to have a look. *Husova ulice 20, Staré Město. The palace is open for researchers in the city archives. Trams: 17 & 18 to Staroměstská.*

The Czech Foreign Ministry functions from the Černín Palace

Letohrádek Portheimka (Portheimka Summer Palace)

The lightness and grace of this diminutive Baroque *Lustschloss* are a delight. The architect Kilián Ignác Dientzenhofer built it for his own family in 1729. Its present name recalls a 19th-century owner. Now an art gallery, the oval saloon with frescoed ceiling looks out on what was once a pleasant garden. *Praha 5, Matoušova ulice 9, Smíchov. Tel: 257 099 971. Only open during exhibitions. Metro: Anděl.*

Lobkowický palác (Lobkowicz Palace)

The powerful Lobkowicz family ended up with no fewer than three palaces in Prague, of which this is the most

Detail of window, Portheimka

'Moor' in Czech. The architect, Giovanni Santini-Aichel, created the palace out of three older houses in 1714. All the sculptural decoration is by Ferdinand Brokoff: above the two side doorways are allegories of *Day* and *Night*, while the *Four Corners of the World* are represented on the roof. The building is currently occupied by the Romanian Embassy.
Nerudova ulice 5, Malá Strana. Open: only to those on embassy business. Trams: 12, 20, 22 & 23 to Malostranské náměstí.

stunning – a masterwork by Giovanni Alliprandi (1707), with a further storey added in 1769 by Ignaz Palliardi.

The best view of its Baroque splendour is from the far side of the English landscape garden at the rear (the palace is now the German Embassy, but access to the garden is sometimes possible). David Černý's bizarre sculpture of a gold-painted Trabant bearing the title *Quo Vadis?* is here, commemorating the time in 1989 when hundreds of East Germans occupied the embassy grounds, demanding West German citizenship.
Vlašská ulice 19, Malá Strana. Open: only to those on embassy business. Trams: 12, 20, 22 & 23 to Malostranské náměstí.

Morzinský palác (Morzin Palace)

A striking feature of the Morzin Palace's façade is the two muscle-bound figures of Moors supporting the balcony. This is a reference to the family name, Morzin –

Nosticův palác (Nostic Palace)

The Nostitz family, great patrons and collectors of art in the 17th century, commissioned Francesco Caratti to build this sumptuous palace in 1658.

JIŘÍ Z PODĚBRAD (GEORGE OF PODĚBRADY) – KING OF BOHEMIA 1458–71

The followers of Jan Hus, the religious reformer, were divided between the radical 'Táborites' and the moderate Utraquists.

The greatest leader of the Utraquist faction was George of Poděbrady, who became regent during the minority of King Ladislav. When the latter died in 1457, George of Poděbrady was elected king by the Bohemian Diet. To mark this event a chalice (the Utraquist symbol) was placed on the façade of the Týn Church (*see p128*).

The reign of George of Poděbrady marked the last, albeit glorious, phase of Hussite independence: the king withstood the machinations of the papacy and tried to unite the princes of Europe against increasing Turkish threat. He was the most able leader of his day, and is regarded as one of the greatest heroes of Bohemian history.

Additions and alterations were made by Giovanni Santini-Aichel in the 18th century; Ferdinand Brokoff added statues of Roman emperors. The Nostitz family built up their own picture gallery and a library which still survives. The building is now shared between the Dutch Embassy and the Ministry of Education. Scenes from the film *Amadeus* were shot in the palace's Baroque interiors.

Maltézské náměstí 1, Malá Strana.
Scholars may visit the library.
Trams: 12, 20, 22 & 23 to Hellichova.

Palác pánů z Kunštátu a Poděbrad (Palace of the Lords of Kunštát and Poděbrady)

Few remnants of Romanesque dwellings remain in Europe, but Prague has more than its fair share. The most striking is the Poděbrad Palace, the basement of which retains its original Romanesque cross-vaulting and fireplaces. What now appears to be the cellar was once the ground floor of the house, before street levels were raised during flood protection works in the second half of the 13th century.

The palace was built at the end of the 12th century or the beginning of the 13th for the Lords of Kunštát and Poděbrady. In 1406, according to the city records, the owner was Lord Boczko of Kunštát, the uncle of George of Poděbrady (*see box opposite*), who inherited the building and lived here between 1453 and 1458.

Řetězová ulice 3. Metro: Můstek.

The fortified Powder Tower

Prašná brána
(Powder Tower)

King Vladislav Jagiello laid the
foundation stone for this huge gate-
tower in 1475. It replaced an earlier
gateway at the point where the trade
from the east entered the city. The new
fortification was modelled on the Staré
Město tower at the end of the Charles
Bridge (see pp86–7). For a while the
king had his residence next door to it,
but later the hostility of the Hussite
burghers compelled him to retreat to
the Hradčany.

In the 18th century the tower was
used as a powder magazine, and was
badly damaged when Frederick the
Great attacked the city in 1757. Josef
Mocker conscientiously 're-Gothicised'
it in 1875, when the statues were placed
on the façade.

The tower can be climbed by those
prepared to negotiate the 186 steps for
the view of Staré Město from the top.
*Náměstí Republiky. Open: daily
Mar–Oct 10am–6pm. Admission charge.
Metro: Náměstí Republiky.*

The Baroque façade of the Wallenstein Palace

Thun-Hohenstejnský palác
(Thun-Hohenstein Palace)

This vast palace demonstrates superbly
how rich owners of small plots of land
in Malá Strana relentlessly extended
their residences by buying up their
less wealthy neighbours. The present
building dates from 1726 and was
designed by Giovanni Santini-Aichel.
The eagles with outstretched wings over
the entrance (by Matthias Braun) are
the heraldic birds of the Kolowrat
family, who originally built the palace.
The Thun-Hohensteins inherited it
only in 1768. The Italian Embassy now
occupies the building.
*Nerudova ulice 20, Malá Strana.
Open: only to those on embassy
business. Trams: 12, 20, 22 & 23 to
Malostranské náměstí.*

Valdštejnský palác
(Wallenstein Palace)

Albrecht von Waldstein (in English
'Wallenstein') was one of the greatest
opportunists in history. Although he
came of Protestant stock, he served the
Habsburgs in the Thirty Years War,
rising swiftly to become commander of
the imperial armies. Having amassed a
gigantic fortune, he decided to build
the grandest palace in Prague, and

demolished a large slice of the Lesser Quarter to do so. The resulting palace remained in the hands of the Wallenstein family until 1945.

The Wallenstein Palace was built between 1624 and 1630 to plans by Andrea Spezza. It encompassed five courtyards and a spectacular garden, and was surrounded by a high wall. The most attractive part of the whole complex is the graceful Renaissance loggia at the west end of the garden, built by Giovanni Pieroni. It is decorated with stucco and frescoes depicting the Trojan War by Baccio Bianco. Bianco also pandered to Wallenstein's taste for self-glorification by painting a fresco inside the palace showing him as the god Mars gliding above the clouds in his victory chariot.

The building's main façade occupies a whole side of Valdštejnské náměstí, but its serried banks of windows and three storeys are more formidable than pleasing. The overall design, which mingles late Renaissance and early Baroque features, seldom achieves the harmonious elegance of later Baroque architecture in Prague.

Niccolò Sebregondi laid out the gardens, at the far end of which is a large Baroque riding school. The garden boasts bronzes by the Dutch artist Adam de Vries, and has a grotto with tufa stalactites at its north end.

The palace now serves as the upper house of the Czech Parliament, the Senate.

Valdštejnské náměstí 4, Malá Strana. Open: Sat & Sun 10am–5pm. Free admission. Trams: 12, 20, 22 & 23 to Malostranské náměstí.
Metro: Malostranská.

Prague Castle looms over the Wallenstein Palace

Patrician and burgher houses

In the Middle Ages, house owners in Prague began the practice of identifying their properties by means of ornamental symbols, wall paintings or, simply, everyday objects attached to the façade. Trade premises would also be appropriately decorated (for example, the violin-maker's house on Nerudova boasts a detailed relief of three violins; and above the door of a former tavern on Husova, two figures are shown carrying a vast bunch of grapes on a pole).

In the 18th century, Maria Theresa introduced the so-called *Konskriptions-nummern* (conscription numbers) for houses, not only to rationalise the addresses of city dwellers, but also to facilitate the systematic checking of army conscription lists.

Despite the introduction of house numbers, many picturesque signs still survive. Most date from Baroque times, although some go back even earlier. The houses described below (five out of many such) have retained their decorative idiosyncrasies. Only those that are restaurants or partly shops may be visited inside.

Dům u dvou zlatých medvědů (House at the Two Golden Bears)

The Renaissance portal of this house has been preserved, but otherwise its aspect is neoclassical, following rebuilding in 1800. Above the lintel are two stone bears (originally gilded). Animals (apparently often chosen at random) were popular motifs for house signs.

Kožná ulice 1, Staré Město.
Metro: Můstek.

Dům u Samuela (At Samuel's)

This originally Gothic, later 'Baroquised', house is situated in the pedestrian zone just below Václavské náměstí (Wenceslas Square). It takes its name from the relief on the corner of the building that shows the biblical King David as a child being anointed as future leader of his people by the prophet Samuel.

Na můstku 4, Staré Město.
Metro: Můstek.

Dům u tří pštrosů (House at the Three Ostriches)

The sign for this house was an advertisement: the 17th-century owner traded in ostrich feathers! Baroque alterations to the building were made in 1657, when the gables were added. An Armenian named Deodatus Damajan may have founded Prague's first coffee house here in the 18th century, and long before that there was a restaurant on the ground floor (as there still is). In 1976 a luxury hotel was added to the facilities. *Dražického náměstí 12. Malá Strana. Trams: 12, 20, 22 & 23 to Malostranské náměstí.*

Dům u zlatého jelena (House at the Golden Stag)

The 'golden stag' here is a spectacular sculptural group above the portals, the work of Ferdinand Brokoff. It shows St Hubert kneeling before an amiable-looking deer: according to legend, St Hubert went hunting on Good Friday and encountered a stag with a golden crucifix lodged in its antlers. This was taken as a warning that he should repent his sacrilegious disregard of a holy day. The Baroque house was built by Kilián Ignác Dientzenhofer in 1726.
Tomášská ulice 4, Malá Strana.

Trams: 12, 20, 22 & 23 to Malostranské náměstí. Metro: Malostranská.

Rottův dům (Rott House)

The cellars of this house still have their Gothic vaulting, and follow the foundations of a Romanesque dwelling on this site. A printshop situated here produced Prague's first printed Bible in 1488. The present neo-Renaissance aspect of the building is the result of alterations made in 1890, when it was owned by an iron merchant named Rott (his name is blazoned across the façade). The front wall was painted with decorative foliage and vignettes by Mikoláš Aleš. Notable are the charming emblematic figures for agriculture and the crafts, whose iron tools were Rott's stock in trade.
Malé náměstí 3, Staré Město. Trams: 17 & 18. Metro: Staroměstská.

Patrician and burgher houses

The front of the Rottův dům is decorated with murals and cartoons by Mikoláš Aleš

Baroque Prague

In the 17th and 18th centuries, the face of Prague changed, reflecting the triumph of the Habsburg dynasty, and of Catholicism in Bohemia. The Baroque style was the official stamp placed on the city by the victors in the struggle for the nation's body and soul.

Baroque architecture still dominates the historic areas of Prague, especially Malá Strana and Hradčanské náměstí. Here the nobility built their fabulous palaces, competing with each other and the emperor in displays of wealth and splendour. Baroque forms were imported from Italy, and, at first, chiefly Italian architects were used.

The Catholic nobility's power and privilege were underlined by the allegorical sculptures of mythological heroes that ornamented the façades and gardens of their palaces. Atlas figures support their splendid

The façade of the Clam-Gallas Palace

entrances, and representations of Hercules triumphant against his foes embellish many stairways or avenues.

Similarly, the magnificent Baroque churches are symbols of the Catholic Church's triumphant Counter-Reformation that followed the defeat of the Protestant cause at the Battle of the White Mountain in 1620.

Prague produced some great Baroque masters, although they were nearly all of foreign origin (František Kaňka is one notable exception). Christoph Dientzenhofer and his son Kilián Ignác were Germans, Jean-Baptiste Mathey came from France, and Giovanni Santini-Aichel was Italian. The prolific Dientzenhofers built the loveliest of Prague's Baroque churches – including the two St Nicholases on Malostranské náměstí and Staroměstské náměstí – as well as many secular buildings. Catholic orders (especially the Jesuits) poured money into religious architecture, and dozens of Gothic churches up and down the land were 'Baroquised'.

Cupolas, towers, terraced gardens, pathos-ridden gesticulating statues – all these conjure a vision of a city once suffused with religious fervour, but which was, simultaneously, the playground of mighty princes.

Prague's houses and churches are rich in Baroque decoration

Petřín (Petřín Hill)

Petřín Hill, an eastern outrider of the White Mountain, was made into a public park in the 19th century. In 1901, it was linked to the Kinsky Gardens by a gap in the Hunger Wall.

According to the 11th-century chronicler Cosmas of Prague, Petřín derives its name from the Latin *petrus* ('stone'); the city did once get most of its building material from here. Later, it was covered with vineyards, and is today a tranquil wooded park with winding paths that attracts Praguers of all ages to walk here in spring when its orchards are in blossom.

Lanová dráha (funicular railway)

The funicular carries you up to the sights of Petřín. On the way it stops at

The Calvary Chapel nestles among the wooded slopes of Petřín Hill

the Nebozízek café and restaurant, which takes its name from the vineyard originally here; its terrace offers good views of the city, and the restaurant serves excellent game dishes.
Open: Apr–Oct daily 9am–11.30pm, Nov–Mar daily 9am–10pm. Trams: 6, 9, 12, 20, 22 & 23 to Újezd. Small charge (one 15-minute public transport ticket).

Petřínská rozhledna (Petřín Tower)

Atop the hill is a scaled-down copy of the Eiffel Tower in Paris, made for the Prague Industrial Exhibition of 1891. There are 299 steps to the viewing platform, and no lift, but the view is worth it – you can see the Krkonoše Mountains on a clear day.
Tel: 257 320 112. Open: 10am–5pm, summer until 10pm. Admission charge.

Kostel svatého Vavřince na Petříně (Church of St Lawrence on Petřín)

The Germans call Petřín 'Laurenziberg' after the man to whom this church is dedicated, whose Romanesque forebear is first mentioned in records of 1135. Kilián Ignác Dientzenhofer and Ignác Palliardi rebuilt it in Baroque style between 1735 and 1770. St Adalbert, the martyred 10th-century Bishop of Prague, is commemorated by a statue, an altar painting and a ceiling fresco depicting him founding the church.

Nearby are Stations of the Cross, culminating in a Calvary Chapel with 19th-century sgraffiti by Mikoláš Aleš. *Closed to the public.*

Bludiště ('Mirror Maze')

An odd-looking pavilion near St Lawrence contains a labyrinth of mirrors. At the end of this is a diorama showing Prague students resisting the onslaught of the Swedes in the invasion of 1648.
Open: Nov–Mar Sat & Sun 10am–5pm, Apr daily 10am–7pm, May–Aug daily 10am–10pm, Sept daily 10am–8pm, Oct Sat & Sun 10am–6pm. Admission charge.

Štefánikova hvězdárna (Štefánik Observatory)

The Astronomical Institute of the Czech Academy of Sciences is based here, and amateurs are allowed to look through the telescopes. The most modern is a 40cm (16-inch) Zeiss, but the older instruments, affectionately known as 'The King' and 'The Comet Finder', are still in use. *The Observatory's opening times are incredibly complicated. It is best to*

HOW TO GET THERE

Access to Petřín Hill: by funicular from the station above Újezd (trams 12, 20, 22 & 23); from the gardens of Strahov Monastery (tram 22 to Pohořelec); from Vlašská ulice (trams 12, 20, 22 & 23 to Malostranské náměstí).

ring 257 320 540 if you want to visit. Closed: Mon.

Hladová zed' (Hunger Wall)

Charles IV had this great fortification built between 1360 and 1362, supposedly as a job-creation scheme for the starving unemployed of the city (hence the name). The wall runs down the hill from the border of the gardens of Strahovský klášter (Strahov Monastery) in the northwest to that of the Kinsky Garden in the southeast.

Springtime attraction: the blossom-clad trees of Petřín Hill

Petřín (Petřín Hill)

Obecní dům

The Municipal House

Architecture was one of the expressions of the increasing self-confidence of the Czech nation which they achieved by the last decade of the 19th century. In Bohemia, 'municipal' or 'national' houses sprang up, combining representational, recreational and social facilities.

Naturally, Prague had the biggest and best Municipal House; its full name – *Representační dům hlavního města Praha* (the Central Representation House of the City of Prague) – indicates its aspirations. It was to be the focus of the Czech capital, celebrating the Czech people. It was here that MPs issued the Epiphany Declaration of January 1918, demanding the setting-up of an independent Czechoslovak state.

The site chosen for this display of civic and national pride was very appropriate; it was to be built where the court of the Jagiello kings had stood, next to the 'Powder Tower' (*see p116*). When the tower was built in the 15th century, the municipality had financed that too, and the burghers had inscribed a declaration on it stressing that it was erected 'to the honour . . . of the citizens of the town'; their rulers were expected to get the message. The tower's main architect, Matěj Rejsek, has been remembered with a statue on the nearest corner of the Municipal

House. A competition for the design was won by Antonín Balšánek and Osvald Polívka. Their project was realised in Art Nouveau style (*see pp30–31*) between 1905 and 1911. It was the most ambitious Art Nouveau building in the whole country, and is in superb condition, thanks to immaculate restoration in the 1990s.

The exterior

The façade is a glorious clutter of glass ornament, wrought-iron railings and theatrical statuary. It is topped by a glazed dome, beneath which a huge arched gable frames Karel Spillar's symbolic mosaic *Homage to Prague*.

The interior

All the leading artists of the Czech Secession had a hand in the decoration of the marvellous interior. Immediately to your right is a vast French restaurant with lavish décor: ornamental stucco and huge gilt chandeliers set off the acres of mural with themes such as

Glorious frescoes adorn both the façade and the interior of the Obecní dům

'Hop Growing', 'Viticulture' or 'Prague Welcomes its Visitors'. Across the vestibule to the left is the equally ornate café, dominated at one end by a fountain with a nymph sculpted from Carrara marble by Josef Pekárek.

In the basement are a slightly overpriced beer cellar and wine bar.

First floor

The focal point is the Smetanova síň (Smetana Hall). Here, the composer Bedřich Smetana's emotionally charged

BEDŘICH SMETANA (1824–84)

The 'Father of Czech Music' composed some fine chamber music, as well as numerous operas for the National Theatre, including *The Bartered Bride* and *The Kiss*.

symphonic poem *Má Vlast* (*My Country*) is performed at the beginning of the Prague Spring Festival (*see p154*). The sculptural groups flanking the stage represent Dvořák's *Bohemian Dances* and scenes from Smetana's opera *Vyšehrad*.

The most important of the other rooms is the Primátorský sál, the circular mayoral hall decorated with paintings by Alphonse Mucha, who also designed a pavilion for the Paris World Exhibition of 1900.

Impressive too is the Riegrův sál, with Max Švabinský's large painted panels entitled *Prague Spring*.
Náměstí Republiky 5. Tel: 222 002 111. www.obecnidum.cz.
Open: daily 10am–7pm.
Metro: Náměstí Republiky.

Obecní dům

Staroměstské náměstí

Old Town Square

If Hradčany was the centre of royal authority in Prague, Staroměstské náměstí was the focus of people's power. John of Luxembourg first gave permission for a Town Hall to be built here in 1338, but an independent-minded municipality had existed long before that.

The square had been the focus of trade and exchange in the 12th and 13th centuries. Goods came in from the East through the customs house in Týn Court (*see p132*) and out on the ancient trade route that crossed the Vltava via the old Judith Bridge (*see pp86–7*). Romanesque remains show the existence of a thriving community then. Most of these buildings were rebuilt in the Gothic style, later receiving a Baroque or Renaissance cladding.

Staroměstské náměstí has always been at the heart of Czech identity. After the first defenestration of Prague in 1419 (*see p45*), the ringleader, Jan Želivský, was executed on the square. The rebellious Protestant nobles met the same fate after the Battle of the White Mountain (1620); they are recalled by 27 white crosses set in the paving in front of the Town Hall. The Hussites (*see p39*) had their hour of glory when their candidate, George of Poděbrady, was elected king in the town hall in

1458. Jan Hus himself is honoured with a massive symbolic statue.

In modern times Staroměstské náměstí has again been the setting where history was made. It saw the jubilation that marked the beginning of Communist rule in 1948, the furious protest at its continuing usurpation of power in 1968 and joy at its demise in 1989. It is also the focal point for demonstrations and celebrations today, such as the frequent Czech ice-hockey victories in the world championships, broadcast live in the square.

Staroměstská radnice (Old Town Hall)

At the southwest corner is the Old Town Hall, which has reached its present proportions by steadily swallowing up neighbouring buildings between the 14th and 19th centuries. In the Great Hall are Václav Brožík's heroic representations of the *Election of George of Poděbrady* and *Jan Hus before the Council of Constance,* complementing the patriotic mosaics in the entrance hall. On the southern façade is the famous Orloj (astronomical clock). On the hour, every hour, Christ and the Twelve Apostles emerge, and the skeleton of Death tolls a bell with one hand while holding a sandglass in the other. You can also see a turbaned Turk, a miser and a vain man admiring himself in a mirror. The complicated clockface shows everything from hours and days to equinoxes and phases of the moon.

According to legend, after the astronomer Master Hanuš put the finishing touches to the clock in 1490, the municipality had him blinded so that he would not repeat his achievement elsewhere. Infuriated by this injustice, Hanuš groped his way up the clock tower and ruined the clock mechanism, which refused to function for 80 years.

Tel: 724 508 584. Open: Mon 11am–6pm, Tue–Sun 9am–6pm. Guided tours of the interior every hour, and access up the tower (great view). Admission charge.

Kostel svatého Mikuláše (Church of St Nicholas)

At the northwest corner of the square stands Kilián Ignác Dientzenhofer's marvellously proportioned Baroque church, built for the Benedictines between 1732 and 1735. The interior is less sumptuous than one might expect; much was removed when Joseph II turned it into a warehouse in the late 18th century. Since 1920, it has belonged to the refounded Czech Hussite Church.

Tel: 224 190 991. Open: daily 10am–4pm, except during concerts or church services.

Staroměstské náměstí

The Baroque Church of St Nicholas dominates the square

Palác Kinských
(Kinský Palace)

On the east side of the square is the Kinský Palace, completed in 1765. Franz Kafka attended a school in the palace, and his father kept a haberdashery shop on the ground floor. It houses part of the National Gallery collection, and is the gallery's information centre (including a book and gift shop).

Staroměstské náměstí 12.
Tel: 224 810 758; www.ngprague.cz.
Admission charge for exhibitions.
Open: Tue–Sun 10am–6pm.

Kostel Panny Marie před Týnem
(Church of Our Lady before Týn)

South of the Kinský Palace is the Venetian-style old parish school (Týnská škola). Through the third arch from the left, access is gained to the Týn Church, built by Petr Parléř's workshop in the 14th century. It was once the stronghold of the moderate Hussites known as Utraquists (*see p114*). Their symbol, a huge gilded chalice, hung on the façade until replaced by a Counter-Reformation image of the Virgin Mary (embellished with gold from the chalice).

The ornate interior contains as highlights Baroque paintings over the high altar by Karel Škréta, a medieval *pietà* in the side-chapel at the east end and the tomb of Tycho Brahe on the fourth pier to the right.

Tel: 222 318 186. Call for visiting hours and times of services.

The House at the Unicorn

Dům u jednorožce
(House at the Unicorn)

This building reveals several layers of architecture – Romanesque, Gothic, Renaissance and, finally, a Baroque façade. Bedřich Smetana founded a music school here in 1848.

Staroměstské náměstí 20.
Not open to the public.

Dům u kamenného zvonu
(House of the Stone Bell)

The existence of this remarkable Gothic house (originally Romanesque) was unknown until the 1960s, when a survey revealed the medieval treasure encased in a Baroque shell. It is thought to have been a palace for Queen Elizabeth, wife of John of Luxembourg. Hosts exhibitions of modern art.

Staroměstské náměstí 16. Tel: 224 827 526; www.ghmp.cz. Open: Tue–Sun

10am–6pm & sometimes for evening concerts on the upper floor. Admission charge for exhibitions.

Dům u minuty
(House of the Minute)

Rebuilt in the 17th century in the style of the Lombardy Renaissance, the walls of this house are completely covered with mythological and biblical sgraffiti. *Staroměstské náměstí 2.*
Not open to the public.

Dům u modré hvězdy
(House at the Blue Star)

This historic inn has a Romanesque hall below ground, while the brick arcades are Gothic. The *vinárna* (wine bar) here, U Bindrů, has been in continuous operation since the 16th century; nowadays it's a bit of a tourist trap. Local characters live on in the names of its main dishes, which bear such names as 'Hanuš' (of astronomical clock fame), and 'Mydlář' (the executioner of the Protestant nobles in 1621, much admired for his cool way with an axe). *Staroměstské náměstí 25.*
Open: daily 11am–midnight.

Pomník Jana Husa
(Jan Hus Monument)

On 6 July 1915, the 500th anniversary of the judicial murder of Jan Hus, this vast Art Nouveau monument was unveiled. Ladislav Šaloun's sculpture exudes pathos and patriotism. Hus stands grimly, flanked by 'the defeated' and 'the defiant'. The inscription runs: 'Truth will prevail' – a quotation from Hus's preaching. The monument became a rallying point and emblem of Czech patriotic feeling. For that reason, the Nazis covered it with swastikas in 1939; in 1968, it was draped in black cloth, a sign of mourning for Czech independence crushed by the Soviets.

Staroměstské náměstí

The Kinský Palace, designed by Kilián Ignác Dientzenhofer

Walk: The heart of the Old Town

*This walk through Prague's historic Staré Město (Old Town) offers a kaleidoscopic tour of the Czech core of the city. (*Follow orange numbers on map for route; for green numbers see *Walk pp80–81.)*

Allow about 1¹⁄₂ hours. The point of departure is Staroměstské náměstí (Old Town Square), which is reached on foot from the Staroměstská Metro station.

1 Staroměstské náměstí (Old Town Square)

In the Old Town Square (*see pp126–9*) there are reminders of a Hussite past in the great Kostel Panny Marie před Týnem (Týn Church) at the east end, and the monument to Jan Hus dominating the northern half of the square.

Nearby, Protestant nobles were executed after rebelling against the Habsburgs. In the more recent past, the 1948 Communist takeover was announced by Klement Gottwald to cheering crowds from a balcony of the Palác Kinských (Kinský Palace) on the east side. A later generation threw Molotov cocktails as Soviet tanks advanced into the square in 1968.

Leave the square by Železná and turn right into Havelská.

2 Havelská

On your left is Kostel svatého Havla (St Gall's Church), where early campaigners preached against the abuses of the Catholic hierarchy. Outside, a lively market sells everything from fruit and flowers to wooden toys and leather goods.

Turn left out of Havelská across Uhelný trh, then left into Rytířská.

3 Rytířská

Halfway down the street is the graceful Stavovské divadlo (Estates Theatre), which Miloš Forman chose for scenes for the film *Amadeus,* since it remains exactly as it was on *Don Giovanni*'s first night. As you walk down Ovocný trh beyond the theatre, you will see an ornate Gothic window protruding from the wall of the Karolinum (Charles University, *see pp84–5*). The street ends in Celetná; on the Cubist corner building (No 34) note the petite *Black Madonna,* a survivor from an earlier Baroque building here.

4 Obecní dům

A right turn into Celetná brings you under the medieval Prašná brána (Powder Tower), and then left, into náměstí Republiky, which is dominated by the Art Nouveau Obecní dům (Municipal House, *see pp124–5*). The independence of Czechoslovakia was proclaimed here in 1918.

Turn left up U Obecního domu, right up Rybná and left up Jakubská, passing along the side of the Kostel svatého Jakuba (St James's Church).

5 Kostel svatého Jakuba

One of the loveliest of Prague's Baroque churches (*see p40*), St James's is beloved by the locals for its sung Masses on Sundays. It has stunning frescoes.

At the northern end of Malá Štupartská turn left into Masná, cross Dlouhá and enter Kozí, bearing right into Haštalská, and then turn left into Anežská.

6 Anežská

The Anežský klášter (St Agnes' Convent, *see pp28–9*) is entered through a gate in the wall. It has fine Gothic architecture and a picture gallery.

From St Agnes' Convent head for Na Františku, via U Milosrdných and Kozí. Then walk left along Na Františku to the trams at Právnická Fakulta.

Walk: The heart of the Old Town

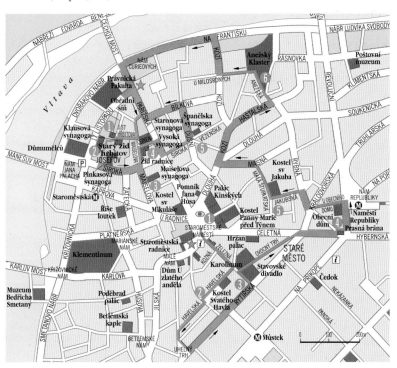

Stavovské divadlo
(Estates Theatre)

This delightful neoclassical theatre was named after the Czech dramatist Josef Týl, but is usually known as the Stavovské divadlo (Estates Theatre), as it belonged to the Bohemian Diet in the early 19th century. Mozart's *Don Giovanni* and *La Clemenza di Tito* were premiered here.

Ovocný trh 1. Tel: 224 901 448.
www.narodni-divadlo.cz.
Ticket sales daily 10am–6pm.
Performances usually begin at 7pm.

Týnský dvůr – Ungelt
(Týn Court or Ungelt)

Týn Court is also known as Ungelt because money (*Geld*) was exchanged and customs dues paid here from medieval times up to 1773. The word *týn* (an enclosed area or courtyard) gave the whole complex of buildings its name. The site was extended to the neighbouring church and school (*see p128*). Exquisitely renovated, it houses some very up-market cafés and shops.

Immediately northeast of Staroměstské náměstí. Metro: Můstek.

Václavské náměstí
(Wenceslas Square)

More of a boulevard than a square, this is the best-known part of Prague, although not the most attractive. The area was once a horse market but has long been the focus for political demonstration. The most dramatic events of the Velvet Revolution took place here, including the historic moment when Václav Havel and Alexander Dubček addressed the crowd from the balcony of the offices of the Socialist Party newspaper (No 36).

The highest end of the square is dominated by the National Museum; below that is Josef Myslbek's monumental equestrian statue of St Wenceslas with the four patron saints of Bohemia (1912). It was here that the student Jan Palach set fire to himself on 16 January 1969.

The buildings

The square is a showcase for 19th- and 20th-century public buildings. There are fine Art Nouveau edifices (the Peterkův dům and the Evropa Hotel – *see p30*), imposing neo-Renaissance blocks and some of Prague's better modern architecture, such as the Bat'a shoe store (No 6). The Hotel Juliš at No 22 was designed by Pavel Janák and (like the shoe store) is a so-called Constructivist work from the 1920s. Also worth a glance is the leisure complex of the Lucerna Palace (No 61), built by Václav Havel's grandfather. The Wiehl House at No 34 is a good example of neo-Renaissance style.

The area encompassing Václavské náměstí, Národní and Na příkopě is the commercial centre of Prague and known as the Golden Cross. Approach is by metro to Muzeum or Můstek.

Vltava bridges

An elaborate lampstand base on the Legií (Legions') Bridge

The Prague section of the Vltava is spanned by 15 bridges (*mosty*). The oldest, Karlův most (Charles Bridge – *see pp86–7*), was also the only one up until 1836.

The great era for bridge-building was the late 19th and early 20th centuries, when the Hlávka, Čech, Palacký, Legions' and Mánes bridges were constructed. The Hlávkův most was named after a rich contractor who financed its construction. Notable are its two allegorical sculptures of Humanity and Work by Jan Štursa. The Čechův most, named after the romantic poet Svatopluk Čech, has attractive early 20th-century decoration and lampposts. The historian František Palacký, the father of the Czech national revival, is honoured in the name of the Palackého most, a bridge crossed by Albert Einstein twice daily as he walked to and from the university.

The Most Legií was inaugurated by Emperor Franz Joseph in 1901, but its name commemorates the Czech Legions who fought against his crumbling empire in World War I. The Mánesův most takes its name from the patriotic painter Josef Mánes, and there is a monument to him standing at the Josefov end.

Bridges seem to be regarded as political barometers, and change their names accordingly. The Mánes Bridge was originally dedicated to the Austrian heir to the throne, Archduke Franz Ferdinand, and the Bridge of the Legions became the Bridge of the First of May under the Communists. Poignantly, the unofficial name for the Bránický most is the 'Bridge of the Intelligentsia', because intellectuals were used as forced labour to build it for the Stalinist regime of the 1950s.

HOW TO GET THERE

Bránický most Trams 3, 17 & 21.
Čechův most Trams 17 & 12.
Hlávkův most Trams 1, 3, 5 & 26.
Metro: Vltavská.
Mánesův most Trams 12, 17, 18, 20, 22 & 23.
Most Legií Trams 6, 9, 18, 21, 22 & 23.
Palackého most Trams 3, 7, 16, 17 & 21.
Metro: Karlovo náměstí.

Walk: Vyšehrad

This walk takes you through the ancient citadel of Vyšehrad on its great rock, and offers Prague's finest views of the Vltava.

Allow 2 hours.

Take the metro (line C) to Vyšehrad. Walk west along the terrace of the ugly modern Prague Conference Centre (or KCP), then enter Na Bučance.

1 Táborská brána (Tabor Gate)

The Tabor Gate of Vyšehrad (meaning 'High Castle') is at the end of the road. Legend says that the Slavic tribes originally settled on this windy outcrop when they reached the Vltava. It was here that Libuše, daughter of an early chieftain, is supposed to have had a vision prophesying the foundation of Prague. However, the archaeological evidence suggests that Hradčany was settled before Vyšehrad.

Continue along V pevnosti.

2 Leopoldova brána (Leopold Gate)

Beyond the Leopoldova brána is the earliest and best preserved of Prague's Romanesque rotundas (Rotunda svatého Martina/St Martin's). It probably served as a cemetery chapel and was built in the 11th century.

Bear left into K rotundě and then right down to the east gate of the Vyšehradský hřbitov (Vyšehrad Cemetery – see p36; opening times vary, but are usually between 8am & 6pm).

3 Vyšehradský hřbitov (Vyšehrad Cemetery)

Leading intellectual figures of the Czech national revival in the 19th century are buried here; but soldiers and politicians are excluded. The most impressive part is the Slavín pantheon commemorating leading figures in the arts.

4 Kostel svatého Petra a Pavla na Vyšehradě (Church of St Peter and St Paul)

A walk through the cemetery brings you to the front of the Kostel svatého Petra a Pavla, which has undergone alteration in every conceivable style since it was built in the 11th century. A Baroque gate to the south leads into a park, presided over by Josef Myslbek's gigantic patriotic sculptures, originally made for the Palackého most (Palacký Bridge). Přemysl and Libuše, founders of the Bohemian dynasty, are on the left.

5 Western bastions

From here a circuit of the western bastions can be made, offering marvellous views of the Vltava streaming sluggishly far below. Note the ruins of a watchtower precariously perched on the almost sheer rock.

Cut back across the park to St Peter and St Paul and continue down to the Cihelná brána (North Gate) of the citadel. To head for home, follow the Přemyslova down towards Na slupi. Otherwise descend towards the town via Vratislavova, then turn right into Hostivítova.

6 Obytný dům (Obyt Flats)

At the corner of Hostivítova and Neklanova (No 30) is Obytný dům, a celebrated Cubist building designed by Josef Chochol (*see pp46–7*). Other such buildings can be seen at Neklanova 2 and at Libušina 3. The latter is Chochol's ambitious Kovarovicova Vila,

with a remarkable façade conceived in diamond shapes and curious zigzag railings round the garden at the rear.

Re-enter Vnislavova and head towards the embankment. Turn right into Rašínovo nábřeží, and a short way along at No 78 is where Václav Havel lived. The Art Nouveau apartment block had been built and owned by his grandfather, a successful contractor at the turn of the 20th century, and has now been returned to the family. You will also see the Fred and Ginger building, frequently known as the Dancing House, at the corner of the Rašínovo nábřeží, designed by Frank Gehry in the mid-1990s.

Retrace your steps along Vnislavova and Neklanova, turning left into Přemyslova. Cross the busy Vnislavova and pass under a crumbling railway bridge, beyond which is Na slupi. Trams for the centre can be boarded here.

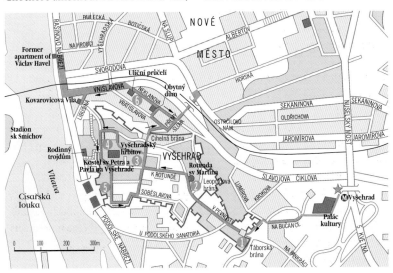

Excursions

Prague is surrounded by a number of historical towns and attractions that make great destinations for a day's excursion. These range from the scenic wine town of Mělník to chilling Terezín, a former Jewish ghetto and concentration camp, and the macabre ossuary at Sedlec.

Český Šternberk (Bohemian Sternberg)

Southeast of Prague is the impressive stronghold of Český Šternberk, built in 1242 on a promontory overlooking the point where the Sázava is joined by its Blanice tributary.

The interior of the castle may be visited as part of a guided tour, and is notable for the Baroque stucco made by Italian craftsmen between 1660 and 1670. Highlights of a visit are the engravings on the staircase depicting scenes from the Thirty Years War, the Yellow Chamber with Carlo Brentano's stucco and a collection of weapons.

The castle lies 45km (28 miles) southeast of Prague off motorway D1. Tel: 317 855 101. www.hradceskysternberk.cz. Open: Apr & Oct Sat, Sun & holidays

Gothic Karlštejn Castle dominates the surrounding countryside

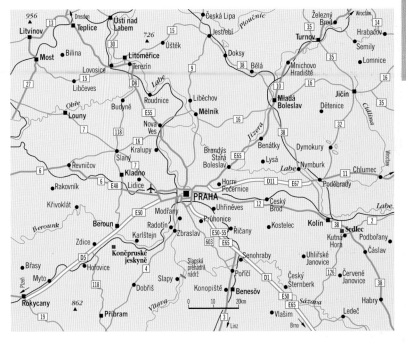

9am–5pm; May & Sept Tue–Sun 9am–5pm; June–Aug, Tue–Sun 9am–6pm. Admission charge.

Hrad Karlštejn (Karlštejn Castle)

The most celebrated Gothic castle in Bohemia was founded by Emperor Charles IV in 1348 and completed by 1357. It was planned as an imperial and Christian sanctuary. On the highest of its three levels is the Chapel of the Holy Rood, which was also a treasury housing the crown jewels of the Holy Roman Empire (now in Vienna) and the Bohemian regalia. The castle's architect is thought to have been Matthew of Arras, who began the building of St Vitus Cathedral.

The castle is approached on foot from the railway station. The car and coach park is 2km (1¼ miles) below. The interior can only be seen with a guided tour. Highlights include the **Audience Hall**, with handsome wooden panelling and a coffered ceiling, and the **Luxembourg Hall**, which contains a model of how the room looked before the 16th century. The **Church of the Virgin Mary** on the second floor of the north tower is notable for the cycle of frescoes showing the emperor receiving

---

HOLIDAY OPENING

Note: if a state holiday falls on Monday, the normal closing day, the castles generally remain open and close on Tuesday instead.

relics from various distinguished donors, and another cycle depicting the Apocalypse. Adjoining the church is **St Catherine's Chapel**, with decoration recalling that of the St Wenceslas Chapel in St Vitus Cathedral.

The recently restored **Kaple svatého Kříže** (Chapel of the Holy Rood) is the high point of the tour. Its 6m (20ft) thick walls are encrusted with 2,200 semi-precious stones, and lined by 128 wooden panels painted by the outstanding court painter Master Theodoric.

Trains leave for Karlštejn from Smíchovské nádřaží in Prague every hour; the journey takes about 45 minutes. By road it is 28km (17 miles) to the southwest. Tel: 311 681 695. www.hradkarlstejn.cz. Castle open:

Tue–Sun, Mar 9am–3pm; Apr & Oct 9am–4pm; May, June & Sept 9am–5pm; July & Aug 9am–6pm; Nov & Dec 9am–3pm. Admission charge (higher for foreigners).

Zámek Konopiště (Konopiště Castle)

This magnificent but gloomy Gothic and Renaissance hunting chateau was acquired in 1887 by Archduke Franz Ferdinand d'Este, the heir to the imperial throne. In 1907 he employed an English botanist to cross-breed roses at Konopiště to produce a black variety – this provoked Delphic warnings about black roses bringing war and death. It apparently took the botanist until 1914 to cultivate the rose. That same year Franz Ferdinand was assassinated in Sarajevo, leading to World War I.

The car park is 2km (1¼ miles) below the castle. You enter through the east tower and walk through a Baroque gateway by F M Kaňka with statues by Matthias Braun. The impressive moat is now perambulated by languid peacocks, but in Franz Ferdinand's day it was occupied by bears.

The guided tours include the St George's Museum, some fine furniture, Habsburg memorabilia and the royal bathroom. The weapons collection is one of the biggest in Europe, with a number of historically important items.

The 90-hectare (222-acre) park is well worth visiting and has an attractive rose garden, a deer park and a lake.

Mělník Castle overlooks the River Labe (Elbe)

Weather-beaten Baroque statues add to the romantic atmosphere.

Konopiště is 50km (31 miles) south of Prague. Tel: 317 721 366. www.zamek-konopiste.cz. Open: Apr & Oct Tue–Fri 9am–3pm, weekends to 4pm; May–Aug Tue–Sun 9am–5pm, Sept Tue–Sun 9am–4pm. Admission charge. A train runs from Praha hlavní nádraží to nearby Benešov (2km/1¼ miles). Alternatively, take a bus from Florenc terminal or Roztyly metro station.

Zámek Křivoklát (Křivoklát Castle)

Ancient Křivoklát is perched on a ledge jutting out of the forests above a tributary of the River Berounka. The castle was first mentioned in records of the year 1110, and became a Přemyslid residence from the reign of Otakar II (1252–78). Much of what is now to be seen is the result of late Gothic reconstruction under the Jagiello king Vladislav II (*see p61*) in the late 14th century. Rudolf II's English alchemist, Edward Kelley, imprisoned here, may have died leaping from a tower window in an attempt to escape.

The castle tour takes about an hour, and is well worth it for the remarkable Gothic architecture, the paintings and sculptures, the chapel and the library.

46km (29 miles) west of Prague. Tel: 313 558 440. www.krivoklat.cz. Open: May–Aug Tue–Sun 9am–5pm; Apr & Sept Tue–Sun 9am–4pm; Oct Tue–Sun 9am–3pm; Nov & Dec Sat & Sun 9am–3pm. Admission charge. Trains

Křivoklát Castle above the River Berounka

run from Smíchovské nádraží to Beroun, where you must change for Rakovník.

Mělník

The wine-producing town of Mělník has a delightful position overlooking the confluence of the Vltava and Labe (Elbe) rivers. The surrounding vineyards were first planted by Charles IV, who brought French wine expertise to the region.

Sights in the town include the Gothic church, the former Lobkowicz Castle, which houses a collection of Baroque paintings, and a Regional Museum. Ideally, you should time a visit to include a meal, which can be enjoyed on the terraces overlooking the rivers. This may also provide an opportunity

to sample the local wine, of which the Tramín is particularly good.
32km (20 miles) north of Prague. Lobkowicz Castle. Tel: 315 622 121. Open: daily 10am–5pm. Admission charge. The bus service from Praha-Holešovice takes about one hour.

Kutná Hora (Kuttenberg)

The name of Bohemia's one-time second-largest city (now a UNESCO World Heritage Site) means 'mining mountain', a reference to the deposits of silver and copper ore on which its prosperity was founded. The mines were vigorously exploited from the late 13th century, bringing a rapid increase in wealth, and attracting miners (chiefly Germans) from outside Bohemia. The royal mint was founded here at the beginning of the 14th century, and experts from Florence produced the *pražské groše* (Prague Groschen), a silver coin regarded as sound currency all over Central Europe for several centuries.

The prosperity of Kutná Hora lasted until the mid-16th century. Dwindling reserves and flooding put paid to the mining, and the town rapidly fell into decline.

HOW TO GET THERE

Kutná Hora is 68km (42 miles) east of Prague. Many buses run from the Želivského or Florenc terminals in Prague and take about 1–1½ hours. Trains run infrequently from Masarykovo or Hlavní nádraží, but the town's main station is a long way from the sights.

Church statuary, Kutná Hora

Alchemy Museum

The museum displays the rich history of Czech alchemy and its relationship with mining and metallurgic traditions.
Paleckého náměstí 377. Tel: 327 511 259. www.alchemy.cz. Open: Apr–Oct 10am–5pm, Nov–Mar 10am–4pm. Admission charge.

Chrám svaté Barbory (Cathedral of St Barbara)

This great Gothic cathedral was financed by the miners and dedicated to their patron saint. Building, initiated by Petr Parléř in the late 14th century, was halted by the Hussite wars. At the end of the 15th century, two of the greatest architects of Prague, Matthias Rejsek and Benedikt Rejt, produced the marvellous late Gothic vaulting inside. There are frescoes showing work in the mint (in the Chapel of the Mintmen), and toiling miners (in the ambulatory).
Tel: 327 512 115. Open: Jan–Apr & Oct–Dec daily 10am–4pm, May–Sept 10am–5.30pm. Admission charge.

Czech Silver Museum
(Mining Museum)

The display rooms of this museum are in the Renaissance house of one John Smíšek, who became rich by exploiting a private (and illegal) mine in the 15th century. Most visitors head for the medieval mine behind the building. At the entrance to the 250m (820ft) of tunnels is a *trejv*, or horse-drawn hoist.

Barborská ulice 28. Tel: 327 512 159. Open: Apr & Oct Tue–Sun 9am–5pm, May, June & Sept Tue–Sun 9am–6pm, July & Aug Tue–Sun 10am–6pm, Nov Sat–Sun 10am–4pm. Admission charge.

Vlašský dvůr (The Italian Court)

Wenceslas II's mint – known as the Italian Court, after the king's Florentine advisers – later became a royal residence. The bricked-up outlines of the mintmen's workshops can still be seen, together with the chapel and parts of the former palace. Across the square to the west is the Gothic Chrám svatého Jakuba (Cathedral of St James), built in 1420 with a Baroque interior.

Havlíčkovo náměstí. Tel: 327 512 873. Open: daily, summer 9am–6pm; winter 10am–4pm. Admission charge.

Other sights worth a visit include Matthias Rejsek's magnificent **Stone Fountain** (1495) in Husova ulice, and the **Kamenný dům** (Stone House) off Hornická ulice, with its richly decorated front. The rooms of this Gothic burgher's house can be visited.

Sedlec

Three kilometres (2 miles) to the north of Kutná Hora is Sedlec, where the star attraction is the Cistercian *kostnice* (ossuary). In the 19th century, František Rint used its approximately 40,000 bones to create what must be one of Europe's most macabre spectacles – an interior decorated with a 'chandelier', 'bells', 'urns', even a Schwarzenberg 'coat of arms', all made from human bones.

www.kostnice.cz. Ossuary open: daily, summer 8am–6pm; winter 9am–noon, 1–4pm. Admission charge. Buses: 1 & 4 from Kutná Hora to Sedlec.

The Cathedral of St Barbara, the patron saint of miners, in Kutná Hora

Lidice

The village of Lidice was razed to the ground by the Nazis on 10 June 1942 in revenge for the assassination of the governor of Bohemia, Reinhard Heydrich, by the Czech resistance. In the village there is a small **Memorial Museum**, and a Rose Garden of Friendship and Peace planted in 1955.

22km (14 miles) northwest of Prague. Lidice Museum. Tel: 312 253 063. www.lidice-memorial.cz.
Open: daily Apr–Oct 9am–6pm, Nov–Mar 9am–4pm.
Regular bus service from Prague to Kladno via Lidice from Praha-Dejvice.

Terezín

Northwest of Prague, in former Sudetenland, Joseph II built a fortified 'town' – in reality, a barracks and prison – in 1780, and named it

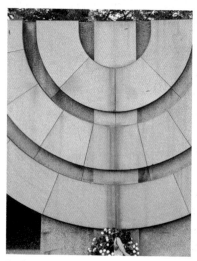

Sombre monument to the Holocaust, Terezín

'Theresienstadt' after his mother, Maria Theresa. In June 1942, the inhabitants were driven out by the Nazis, and the main part of it was turned into a ghetto for Jews.

The Nazis used Terezín for propaganda, allowing the doomed Jews to pursue cultural activities such as music and drama, and building gleaming facilities to show visitors from the Red Cross. The **Ghetto Museum** has an informative (and harrowing) display, including clips from the propaganda film *Hitler Gives the Jews a Town*.

On the other side of the river that divides the town, the **Malá Pevnost** (**Lesser Fortress**) may also be visited. A prison under the Habsburgs (Gavrilo Princip, who assassinated Archduke Franz Ferdinand at Sarajevo in 1914, languished here), it was later used as a concentration camp and extermination centre. There is an exhibition in the former house of the camp commandant. You can also tour the cells.

60km (37 miles) northwest of Prague. Ghetto Museum. Tel: 416 782 225. www.pamatnik-terezin.cz. Open: daily 9am–6pm (5.30pm in winter). Closed: 24–26 Dec & 1 Jan.
The Malá Pevnost: Tel: 416 782 225. www.pamatnik-terezin.cz. Open: daily 9am–6pm (4.30pm in winter). Terezín is 1½ hours by bus from Florenc bus terminal. Weekly tours also leave from Josefov (ask at the ticket office of the State Jewish Museum) and are run by many guided tour companies in Prague.

The tower of the Old Town Hall is a commanding presence in Terezín

Getting away from it all

Most visitors to Prague come to enjoy the delights of city life, but those who venture beyond the end of the city's metro lines discover a whole new side to Prague as the city melts away into the wooded hills of Central Bohemia. Even within the city centre, hopping onto one of the islands in the River Vltava, taking a boat trip up or down stream or whiling away an afternoon in a leafy Prague park are ideal ways to unwind and escape the hubbub of the capital, at least for a while.

Boat trips on the Vltava

From April to September, as long as there is enough water, excursions run both north and south on the Vltava. To the north, they go as far as Roztoky (1 hour 20 minutes), and to the south as far as Štěchovice (3 hours) and Slapy Dam (4 hours). Shorter trips offer a 'panorama of Prague' (50 minutes to 2 hours), and a paddle steamer also operates occasionally. Check details with the Prague Information Service (*www.pis.cz*).

A favourite destination for Praguers who want to get away from it all is **Slapská přehradní nádrž** (Slapy Dam), reached via a picturesque 33km (21 mile) stretch of the Vltava Valley. The 65m (213ft) high dam was built in 1954, and has 40km (25 miles) of reservoir stretching behind it which is a paradise for watersports and fishing.

Bílá Hora (White Mountain)

On the western outskirts of Prague is the White Mountain, where the most decisive battle of Bohemian history was fought on 8 November 1620. On this limestone plateau, the Protestant mercenaries of Bohemia, under Count Thun, were decisively defeated by an imperial Catholic army under Maximilian of Bavaria. The elected Bohemian king (Frederick of the Palatinate) fled, opening the way to three centuries of Habsburg rule. Czechs see this date as marking the end of their independence (not regained until 1918), and the beginning of *temno* (darkness). A small monument marks the site of the battle.

Nearby, to the south, is the **Chrám Panny Marie Vítězné** (Church of Our

BOAT TRIPS

Excursion boats are run by Pražská Paroplavební Společnost (PPS) and leave from the mooring at Palackého most (*tel: 224 931 013; www.paroplavba.cz*). The nearest metro station is Karlovo náměstí. Lines run to Slapy, Štechovice, Stromovka (and the Zoo). There are organised sightseeing cruises as well as boats for hire.

Lady Victorious), built as a chapel in 1622, and rebuilt as a pilgrimage church between 1704 and 1714. Its interior has fine Baroque frescoes.

The monument is further to the west and along Nad višňovkou; the church is next to the tram stop. Trams: 22 & 25 up to end stop at Bílá Hora. This trip can easily be combined with a visit to the Letóhrádek Hvězda (see below).

Koněpruské jeskyně – Český kras (Koněprusy Caves and the Bohemian Karst)

The Bohemian Karst is a protected ecological area, rich in rare flora, but most visitors go to see the stalactite and stalagmite limestone caves. Since their discovery in 1950, 800m (2,625ft) of labyrinthine chambers have been made accessible to the public.

Another exciting discovery was the remains of an illegal mint dating from the second half of the 15th century (there is a small exhibition about it).

50 minutes by train from Praha Hlavní nádraží. http://jeskyne.cesky-kras.cz/english. Open: Apr–Oct Tue–Sun. Admission charge. The visit could be combined with an excursion to Karlštejn; from Srbsko (one stop beyond Karlštejn on the railway), a yellow-marked path leads to the caves (about 3km/2 miles). A bus connects them with the station at Beroun.

Kunratický les (Kunratice Woods)

This extensive area of pleasant woodland southeast of the city is criss-crossed with asphalted paths. A moufflon herd is said to run wild here; there is a mini-zoo at the forester's hut with a few wild boar, deer and pheasants.

You can walk to the ruin of Nový hrad, known as the 'Stone of Wenceslas' because Wenceslas IV built it as a hunting lodge. Supposedly, it was here, in 1419, that the king had a fatal stroke on hearing of the defenestration of Catholic councillors. There is a restaurant named after the choleric king, U krále Václava IV.

On the west side of the woodland flows the River Kunratice. Several of its pools make informal bathing beaches, mostly around Šeberák. Near here the first nude beach was instituted when such things were still considered extremely daring.

Metro: (line C) to Roztyly.

Letohrádek Hvězda (Hvězda Summer Palace)

The Imperial Governor of Bohemia, Ferdinand of Tyrol, himself designed this remarkable Renaissance country house. It was built in the form of a six-pointed star between 1555 and 1557 by Italian architects, and has preserved its original aspect with the exception of the roof, which is 18th-century. Especially attractive features inside are the stucco reliefs of scenes from classical mythology and Roman history. The gods personifying the planets named after them form the focal points on the ceilings of individual rooms.

In the cellars are tableaux with explanatory texts about the defenestration of Prague and the Battle of the White Mountain.

After World War II, the castle was sensitively restored by Pavel Janák and now houses an exhibition on the development of the building over the centuries and a scale model of the Battle of the White Mountain.

Open: Apr & Oct Tue–Sun 10am–5pm, May–Sept Tue–Sun 10am–6pm. Admission charge. Trams: 15, 22 & 25 to Vypich (beyond Břevnov).

Průhonice

Most visitors to the town of Průhonice, on the southeast periphery of Prague, are drawn by the vast and marvellous landscaped botanical park. It has 700 different plants and shrubs, including

Signposts direct walkers in the woods

alpine species and rhododendrons. (The castle, now a botanical research institute, is closed to visitors.)

A regular bus service to Průhonice runs from Opatov metro. By car, turn off the D1 motorway about 10km (6 miles) after leaving the city.

Vltava islands

Ten islands remain from roughly twice that number before the regulation of the Vltava in the late 19th century. The most picturesque is **Kampa**, an island only by virtue of the millstream that separates it from the Malá Strana bank.

Opposite Vyšehrad are **Císařská louka** (the Emperor's Meadow) on the Smíchov side (a venue for watersports and camping) and **Veslařský ostrov** off the Vyšehrad/Podolí shore (the haunt of sailors and skullers). **Slovanský ostrov** (between Jiráskův most and most Legií) has rowing boats for hire in summer. All the islands are accessible on foot.

Výstaviště and Stromovka Park

The Holešovice district of Prague has an extensive exhibition area (Výstaviště) for which remarkable buildings were designed in 1891 (*see pp30–31*). Apart from the regular fairs and exhibitions held here, the place is known for its funfair (**Dětský svět**), its **Planetarium** and the **Maroldovo panoráma**, an 1898 diorama of the Battle of Lipany (1434).

The leafy Stromovka Park, stretching to the west of Výstaviště, was planted on the orders of Rudolf II in 1593, and has an artificial lake. You can cross the park and river, and reach both Troja castle and the zoo from here (allow 45 minutes at least).

Výstaviště. Open: Tue–Thur 2–10pm, Sat & Sun 10am–10pm. Metro: Nádraží Holešovice. Trams: 5, 12, 14, 15 & 17 to Výstaviště.

Planetarium: generally open 8am–6pm, but hours vary.

Maroldovo panoráma. Open: Tue–Fri 2–5pm, Sat & Sun 10am–5pm. Closed in winter.

The landscaped park at Průhonice

Shopping

Prague boasts an ever-growing range of boutiques, shops and hypermarkets. International brand names in food, furniture and clothing are certainly in great evidence. Credit cards are widely accepted (MasterCard and Visa, in particular) in most stores, and you can use almost any card at the many ATMs.

WHAT TO BUY

There are a number of items for which Bohemia is famous, particularly glassware. Embroidered textiles are also worth considering, as are hand-crafted puppets and wooden toys.

Antiques

Alma Mahler Antique
One of Prague's largest antiques dealers with two outlets.
Valentinská 7, Staré Město.
Tel: 222 325 865 and
Radnické Schody 9, Hradčany.
Tel: 220 513 869.
Bohemia Crown Antique
Korunní 8, Vinohrady.
Tel: 222 514 191.

Foreign-language bookshops

All the following stock books in English:
Anagram
Týn 4, Praha 1. Tel: 224 895 737.
Big Ben Bookshop
Malá Štupartská 5, Praha 1.
Tel: 224 826 565.

The Globe
Pštrossova 6, Praha 1.
Tel: 224 934 203.
Shakespeare and Sons
U Lužického semináře 91, Praha 1.
Tel: 257 531 894.

Department stores

Bilá Labut'
Na Poříčí 23, Praha 1.
Tel: 224 811 364.
Open: Mon–Fri 9am–8pm, Sat 9am–6pm, Sun 10am–6pm.
Kotva
Náměstí Republiky 8, Praha 1.
Tel: 224 801 111.
Open until 8pm except weekends.
Palladium
Prague's newest temple to consumer choice with five glittering floors containing 170 outlets.
Náměstí Republiky 1, Praha 1.
Tel: 225 770 250.
www.palladiumpraha.cz.
Open: Mon–Sat 9am–10pm, Sun 9am–9pm. Metro: Náměstí Republiky.

Glass

Bohemia-Moser

Moser is a top-quality name in Bohemian glass. Mailing service.
Na příkopě 12, Praha 1. Tel: 224 211 293. Also on Malé náměstí 11.

Cristallino

Glass, porcelain and jewellery.
Celetná 12, Praha 1. Tel: 224 225 173.

Music

Bontonland

Václavské náměstí. Tel: 224 473 080.

Oldies But Goodies

New CDs as well as Eastern European relics on vinyl.
Prokopská 3, Malá Strana. Open: Mon–Fri 11am–6pm. Closed: weekends.

UniJazz

Alternative music shop and club.
Jindřišská 5, Praha1. Tel: 222 240 901. Open: Mon–Fri 2–6pm.

Souvenirs

Blue Praha

Sells glass, gifts, T-shirts and cards.
Malé náměstí 14, Praha 1 (and branches in the centre). Tel: 224 216 717.

Botanicus

High-quality, organic, handmade soaps, oils, candles and creams.
Ungelt Týnský dvůr 3, Praha 1 (and other centres). Tel: 234 767 446.
www.botanicus.cz

Manufaktura cosmetics

Handmade toys, traditional fabrics, metal ornaments, and other reasonably priced and authentic gift items.

Melantrichová 17, Praha 1 (and other branches). Tel: 221 632 480.
www.manufaktura.biz

Clothes

Bohème

Good selection of Czech knitwear, leather goods and accessories.
Dušní 8, Praha 1. Tel: 224 813 840.
www.boheme.cz

Tatiana

Upmarket style.
Dušní 1, Praha 1. Tel: 224 813 723.
www.tatiana.cz

Perfumeries

Local perfumeries include FAnn, Body Basics and Rossmann. Their branches are dotted all over town.

Try Botanicus for luxury soaps and candles

Bohemian glass

Bohemia means excellent dumplings, beer and glass. The last two are traditionally inseparable, since the Bohemian glassmakers have probably always needed constant rehydration as they worked at the glass furnaces. Owners were obliged to brew good beer on their estates to keep their glass-making tenants happy, which is doubtless the reason why the quality of both glass and beer has never declined.

The tradition of glassmaking in Bohemia goes back at least to 1414, and possibly as far back as the Celts. The process went on deep in the forests, which supplied the wood for the furnaces, and glassmakers moved from place to place as wood stocks were exhausted. In the 17th century, the trade separated – makers of raw glass delivered to specialists who cut, engraved and gilded it. At first, pedlars took the products all over Europe, but by the beginning of the 18th century 'Bohemian Houses' were marketing the famed Czech glass in 38 European ports, as well as America, North Africa and elsewhere.

During the Renaissance, there were gimmicky innovations (drinking vessels that gurgled or whistled as you drained them); the Baroque period was notable for beautiful engraving on a specially strong glass – Bohemian crystal; the 19th century developed brilliantly coloured glazes. The iridescent Art Nouveau glass of the turn of the 20th century is often even more exotic, with its sensuous shapes and metallic lustre.

Almost all antique shops will have a few pieces of decorative historic glass in the window, while a plethora of crystal shops will sell you modern crystal of varying quality. The latest fashion is for 'old-style' glass made to the designs using traditional techniques in North Bohemia – from Roman to Renaissance to the 1920s. You can spot this glass, thanks to its slightly green tinge. Former US President Bill Clinton has quite a collection.

Glassware is found in most antiques shops

Bohemian glassware has been produced in Prague since medieval times

Entertainment

There is a lively art scene in Prague, and plenty of galleries. Exhibitions are held in many historic buildings such as the House of the Stone Bell, and the Kinsky Palace on Staroměstské náměstí.

Art galleries

Dům u Černé Matky Boží
Top contemporary Czech art is regularly shown in this classic Cubist building. *Ovocný trh 18, Praha 1. Tel: 224 211 746. Open: Tue–Sun 10am–6pm.*

Galerie Rudolfinum
Modern, ultra-innovative art. *Alšovo nábřeží 12, Praha 1. Tel: 227 059 309. www.galerierudolfinum.cz. Open: Tue–Sun 10am–6pm.*

Ivana Follova Art and Fashion Gallery
Offers original glass, ceramics and clothes to buy and browse through (as well as designer clothes). *Vodičkova 36, Praha 1. Tel: 296 236 497. www.ifart.cz. Open: daily 10.30am–7pm.*

Mánes Gallery
The moving spirit behind this gallery was the 19th-century history painter Josef Mánes, who founded an Artists' Association in 1887. The modern building overlooking the Vltava was designed by Otakar Novotný and incorporates a café. *Masarykovo nábřeží 250, Nové Město. Tel: 224 930 754. www.galeriemanes.cz. Open: Tue–Sun 10am–6pm. Closed: Mon.*

'Black' theatre, mime, puppetry
There is now a lot to choose from, and some of the shows are devised with the foreign visitor in mind. The mime tradition of Prague is very sophisticated, and the best shows are memorable.

Regular art exhibitions are held at the Emmaus Monastery in Nové Město

Ballet is on offer at the National Theatre (Národní divadlo)

Divadlo Image
Mime and pantomime.
Pařížská 4, Staré Město. Tel: 222 329 191. www.imagetheatre.cz

Divadlo Na zábradlí
Mime shows as well as straight theatre.
Anenské náměstí 5, Praha 1.
Tel: 222 868 870. www.nazabradli.cz

Divadlo Spejbla a Hurvínka
Josef Škupa's famous puppet duo.
Dejvická 38, Praha-Dejvice.
Tel: 224 316 784. www.spejbl-hurvinek.cz

Cinema

The tabloid section of the weekly English-language newspaper *Prague Post* (*www.praguepost.com*) lists films shown in English (foreign films are rarely dubbed into Czech for the cinema). The British Council (*Politických vězňů 13, Nové Město, tel: 221 991 111*) shows English films, and Studio MAT (*on Karlovo náměstí; tel: 224 915 765. www.mat.cz*) shows Czech films with English subtitles from time to time.

Czech cinema is noted for its off-beat humour and deadpan satire. Miloš Forman's early films were examples of this, while the most enchanting of the Czech New Wave films was Jiří Menzel's *Closely Observed Trains* (1966).

MUSIC

Prague is one of the great centres of music-making in Europe (*see pp108–9*). Since 1989, the opportunities for Czech composers and musicians have broadened considerably and excitingly.

ART COLLECTIONS

For the permanent collections of the **National Gallery**, *see pp110–11*. Contemporary Czech art is displayed in the **Museum of Modern and Contemporary Czech Art**, Veletržní Palace, Holešovice.

Bohemian musical tradition is rich in Baroque composers and the 19th-century Romantics. For example, a group called Musica Antiqua Praha specialises in Baroque works played on original instruments. Their repertoire includes items of music from the archives of a 17th-century Bishop of Olomouc in Moravia, discovered by their director, Paul Kliner. The first privately funded ensemble, the Virtuosi di Praga, concentrates on the music of Mozart. If you want to know more about Czech composers, or would like to buy Czech sheet music, try TALACKO, *Rybná 29, Staré Město, www.talacko.cz* (English and Czech-speaking). Music can be heard live at the following venues:

Concert halls
Rudolfinum
Alšovo Nábř 12, Staré Město.
Tel: 227 059 227.
Smetanova síň Obecního domu (Smetana Hall of the Municipal House)
Náměstí Republiky 5, Nové Město.
Tel: 222 002 101.
www.obecnidum.cz
The Bertramka (*Mozartova 169, Smíchov, tel: 257 318 461*) and
Vila Amerika (*Ke Karlovu 20, tel: 224 918 013*) hold regular evening performances of Mozart and Dvořák arias (*see pp106–7*).
Concerts and recitals take place in many of the city's palaces and churches through the year.

PRAGUE MUSIC FESTIVALS

The Pražské Jaro (Prague Spring) traditionally begins with a performance of Smetana's *Má Vlast* (*My Country*), and ends with Beethoven's 9th Symphony. In between is a rich programme of opera, choral works, chamber music, and recitals given by international stars. In July and August, Prague Cultural Summer features music, dance and theatre. Praga Europa Musica in September presents a programme combining aspects of Czech music with music of another European country.
Prague Spring box office, Hellichova 18, Malá Strana. www.festival.cz or www.ticketpro.cz

Folk music
Folklore Garden
Corner of Na Zlíchově and Nad Konečnou. *Tel: 251 552 255.*
www.folkloregarden.cz.
Trams: 12, 14 & 20 to Hlubočepy.

Jazz
Agharta Jazz Centrum
Probably one of Prague's best venues.
Železna 16, Praha 1.
Tel: 222 211 275.
Open: daily 6pm–1am.
U Staré Paní (Jazz Lounge)
Dinner, drinks and jazz. Reservations essential.
Michalská 9, Staré Město.
Tel: 603 551 680.
Open: daily 7pm–2am.
Metropolitan Jazz Club
Swing, ragtime and blues are among the attractions.
Jungmannova 14, Nové Město.
Tel: 224 947 777.
Open: daily 7pm–1am.

The Rudolfinum concert hall

Reduta Jazz Club

A great survivor. Dixieland, swing and modern jazz on offer.

Národní 20, Nové Město.

Tel: 224 933 487. Open: daily 9pm–midnight.

Opera

Národní divadlo (National Theatre)

Opera and theatre performances.

Národní 2, Nové Město.

Tel: 224 901 319.

Státní opera (State Opera)

Opera and ballet.

Wilsonova 4, Nové Město. Tel: 224 227 266.

Stavovske divadlo (Estates Theatre)

Opera, ballet, theatre.

Ovocný trh 1 Praha 1.

Tel: 224 901 448.

Operetta and musicals

Hudební divadlo Karlín (Karlin Music Theatre)

Křižíkova 10, Praha 8.

Tel: 221 868 666.

NIGHTLIFE

The ingredients of Prague nightlife are much the same as elsewhere: ranging from bars, jazz clubs and other live-music venues to floor shows, casinos and discos. To get the latest information on the club scene, grab a copy of Czech-English (free) *Think* (*www.think.cz*), available at most English-language music shops, Radost FX Club and central 'trendy' restaurants, cafés and bars. Otherwise, consult ticket agencies, the *Prague Post* (*www.praguepost.com*), or buy a copy of *Přehled*, a monthly guide to what's on, in Czech, or *Welcome to Prague*, a useful monthly listings guide. Wenceslas Square and Betlemské náměstí have a reputation for prostitution, as well as drunk men on stag-weekends, and you should watch yourself and your valuables at night.

Cabaret, floor shows

Traditional floor shows are held mainly in hotels. Be sure to reserve a table.

Alhambra & Goldfingers (Ambassador Hotel)

Václavske náměstí 5, Praha 1.
Tel: 224 193 111.

Esplanade

Washingtonova 19, Nové Město.
Tel: 224 501 111.

U Fleků

Kitsch tour bus cabaret featuring the tavern's very own troupe who perform everything from polka to Latin.
Křemencova 11, Praha 1.
Tel: 224 934 019.

Casinos

Ambassador

Ambassador Hotel, Václavske náměstí 5, Praha 1. Tel: 224 193 111.
Open: 24 hours.

Casino Atrium

Hilton Hotel, Pobřežní 1, Praha 8. Tel: 224 810 988. Open: daily 2pm–5am.

Casino Palais Savarin

Na příkopě 10, Nové Město. Tel: 224 221 636. Open: daily 1pm–3am.

Hotel Corinthia

Hotel Corinthia Panorama, Milevska 7, Praha 4. Tel: 261 164 061.
Open: 8pm–4am.

Dancing

Akropolis

Arty and ethnic events; very laid-back.
Kubelíkova 27, Praha 3.
Tel: 296 330 911.

Bílý Koníček

Old and new dance hits.
Staroměstské náměstí 20. Tel: 221 421 160. Open: daily 8pm–5am.

Karlovy Lázně

Disco complex.
Smetanovo Nábřeži 198, Praha 1.
Tel: 222 220 502. www.karlovylazne.cz

Lucerna Music Bar

Daily programme starts at 9pm.
New on the Prague scene.
Vodičkova 36, Nové Město.
Tel: 224 217 108. Open: daily 10am–3am.

Radost FX

Veggie café, disco and art gallery.
Bělehradská 120, Praha 2.
Tel: 224 254 776. www.radostfx.cz

Roxy

One of the best funk and techno clubs in town.
Dlouhá 33, Staré Město.
Tel: 224 826 296.

Rock scene and gigs

The best way to catch the latest happenings in the city is to study the

Young musicians provide a classical treat using traditional instruments

listings in the *Prague Post* (weekly) or *Prague Events* (monthly).

Mecca Club

International and local acts perform in this funky ex-warehouse. There is also a restaurant and café.

U Průhonu 3, Praha 7. Tel: 283 870 522. www.mecca.cz. Open: Mon–Thur 11am–11pm, Fri 11am–6pm, Sat 7pm–6am. Closed Sun.

Rock Café

Hard rock and thrash metal. Sometimes live bands. Loud. T-shirts on sale.

Národní 20, Praha 1. Tel: 224 933 947. Open: daily 10am–3am (Sat 5pm–3am, Sun 5pm–1am).

Theatre

Tickets are available at box offices or through ticket agents: PIS at Na příkopě 20, Staroměstské náměstí 1 (*tel: 236 002 569. www.pis.cz*), Mostecká Věž (in summer only), and Mostecká 2, Malá Strana; also at Bohemia Ticket at Na příkopě 16, or Malá náměstí 13, Staré Město (*tel: 224 227 832. www.bohemiaticket.cz*).

The language barrier will block most visitors' appreciation of Czech theatre, though some contemporary dramatists' works are known through translations, most notably Bohumil Hrabal and Václav Havel.

The many small or fringe theatres of Prague put on new work, while the **National Theatre**, Národní 2 (*tel: 224 901 319*), delights audiences by offering classics as well as ballet and opera.

Its Nova Scéna extension stages the multimedia Laterna Magika shows (*see pp104–5*).

Children

Prague is rich in possibilities for keeping children absorbed and contented. There is always plenty going on in Old Town Square (Staroměstské náměstí), and the river is another attraction. Caves, museums, puppets and a funfair also beckon.

You could begin with the all-action astronomical clock in Old Town Square and follow up with a tour of the sewers (entrance to the right of the clock tower). In summer, the square is alive with strolling players, ice-cream vendors, and booths selling food and souvenirs. A miniature train leaves from here and runs along Pařížská, over Cechův most and on to Hradčany. Horse-drawn carriages leave from the square for an hour-long tour of the Staré Město.

Another obvious attraction is the river. Cruises start from Palackého most, Rašínovo nábřeží (*for information call 224 931 013*) and go both upstream and downstream. The longest round-trip lasts more than seven hours, so check timetables and destinations carefully. On a sunny day, fun and exercise may be had by hiring a pedalo from Kampa Island, or the island called Slovanský ostrov or Žofín off Masarykovo nábřeží.

Caves

The stalactite caves of Koněpruské jeskyně in the karst region around Karlštejn offer an exotic alternative excursion. If the children are too small to attempt the 3km (2-mile) walk from Srbsko station, an infrequent bus runs between Beroun and the caves. Beroun is 50 minutes by train from Praha Hlavní nádraží (*see p145*).

Cinema
Multiplex Flóra
Set within the Palác Flóra entertainment and shopping centre are eight cinemas, an IMAX theatre, in-line skating and an indoor play area with a babysitting service.

MUSEUMS

The museums mentioned here are covered in detail with full addresses and opening hours on *pp98–103*; only aspects of specific interest to children are stressed here. Likewise, Koněpruské jeskyně is featured on *p145*, Petřín Hill on *pp122–3*, Výstaviště on *p146*, and cruising on *p144*.

Palác Flóra, Vinohradská 151, Prague 3.
Metro: Flora.

Mirror maze

Petřín Hill is ideal for an excursion
with younger children, involving the
funicular railway from Újezd, the
astronomical observatory, the mini-
Eiffel Tower and the Bludiště (mirror
maze), which never fails to delight.

Museums

The Army Museum in Žižkov (post-
1914) will no doubt fascinate older
children. The view from the museum
(*see p98*) is one of the best in Prague.
The huge equestrian monument of the
Hussite general Jan Žižka, in front of
the museum, is in the *Guinness World
Records* as the largest sculpture in
the world.

The Museum of Flight (*see p98*) is
worth the longish trek, but the National
Technical Museum (*see p102*) is even
more guaranteed to be a hit with the
young. The highlights are the cars, the
motorbikes, the astronomical
instruments and a complete mock-up
of a coal mine (currently closed for
renovation, due to reopen by 2010).

Puppet theatres

Puppetry has a long tradition in the
Czech Republic, and has influenced
puppet theatres the world over. Go back
to puppetry's roots at a Prague theatre.

Divadlo Minor

Continuous programmes for children.
Vodičkova 6, Praha 1. Tel: 222 231 351.
www.minor.cz. Metro: Náměstí Republiky.

Ríše Loutek

Matinée marionette performances.
Žatecká 1. Tel: 222 324 565.
www.riseloutek.cz. Trams 17 & 18.
Metro: Staroměstská.

Theme parks and zoos

Výstaviště

Funfair, big wheel, Planetarium, Sea
World and other attractions.
Praha 7.
Planetarium. Tel: 220 999 001.
www.planetarium.cz. Open: Mon–Thur
8.30am–noon, 1–8pm, Sat & Sun
9.30am–noon, 1–8pm.
Sea World. Tel: 220 103 275.
www.morsky-svet.cz.
Open: daily 10am–7pm.

Zoo Praha

An ever-popular location for a day out.
In Troja, Praha 7. Tel: 296 112 111.
www.zoopraha.cz. Open: daily
9am–7pm, 4pm in winter. Metro:
Nádraží Holešovice, then take
bus No 112.

Puppets to delight the young and old

Sport and leisure

The most passionately followed sports in Prague are football and ice hockey. The latter famously sparked riots in 1969, when the Czech team humiliated the Soviet Union. This was seen as sweet revenge for the Warsaw Pact invasion of the previous year. The Czechs continue to win the World Ice Hockey Championships with almost monotonous regularity.

Billiards

You can play billiards pretty much all over town – look for 'Billiard Club' signs.

Bowling

Hotel Corinthia

Just four lanes (but the ten types of beer are a compensation).
Kongresová 1, Praha 4. Tel: 261 191 151. Open: daily noon–1am. Metro: to Vyšehrad.

RAN Bowling Centre

Eight professional lanes and a well-stocked bar.
V Celnici 10, Praha 1. Tel: 221 033 020. Open: daily noon–2am.

Fitness centres

Fitness centres and gyms have mushroomed in Prague recently. Try:
The World Class Health Academy
Top-class gym and pool, with excellent classes (below the Marriott Hotel).
Millennium Plaza, V Celnici 10, Praha 1. Tel: 221 033 033. Mon–Fri 6am–10pm, Sat & Sun 8am–9pm.

YMCA

Pool, gym and aerobics.
Na Poříčí 12, Praha 1. Tel: 224 875 811. Open: Mon–Fri 6.30am–10pm, Sat & Sun 10am–9pm.

Football (soccer)

The two leading clubs are Sparta Praha and Slavia. Check details at:
www.sparta.cz and *www.slavia.cz*

Golf

Czech golfing opportunities are booming, with superb courses in Karlovy Vary (Carlsbad), Marianské Lázně (Marienbad) and Karlštejn. They also include the country's best indoor facility and driving range. Call the Czech Golfing Association for further details.
Strakonická 2860, Praha 5. Tel: 257 317 865. www.cgf.cz

Horse racing

Steeplechasing and hurdles take place at Velká Chuchle from May to October

on Sunday afternoons; trotting all year round.
Velká Chuchle, Radontínská 69, Praha 5.
Tel: 257 941 431. Admission charge.
Buses: 129, 172, 241, 244 & 255,
from Smíchovské nádraží to Dostihová.

Ice hockey

Catch the professionals at the T-Mobile Aréna (*Za Elektrárnou 419, Praha 7*) or HC Slavia Praha (*Vladivostocká 1460, Praha 10*). *www.hokej.cz*

Ice skating

There are a few rinks, most with erratic opening times.

HC Hvězda Praha

Na rozdílu 1, Praha 6. Tel: 235 352 759.
Open: winter only, Sat & Sun 3–5pm.
Metro: Dejvická, then tram 2, 20 or 26 to Bořislavka.

Zimní Stadión Nikolajka

U Nikolajky 28, Praha 5. Tel: 251 561 269.
Open: winter only, Sat & Sun 1–3.30pm.
Metro: Anděl. Trams: 4, 6, 7, 9, 12 & 14.

Squash

Squash courts are becoming increasingly common. The Squash Centrum is in the heart of Prague, but you can also find courts at Club Hotel Praha and Hotel Corinthia.
Squash Centrum: Václavské náměstí 15, Praha 1. Tel: 224 232 752.

Swimming

Swimming in the River Vltava is not recommended. There are plenty of pools, but not all are as clean as they should be. Those recommended are at: *Plavecký Stadión, Podolská 74, Podolí. Tel: 241 433 952. Open: Mon–Fri 6am–9.45pm. Sat & Sun 6am–10pm. Trams: 3, 7, 16, 17 & 21 to Kublov; also at the YMCA (see opposite).*

Tennis

Czech Lawn Tennis Club

Štvanice ostrov. Tel: 224 810 272. Open: Apr–Oct 6am–dusk. Metro: Florenc.

Tenisový Klub Slavia

Eight floodlit clay courts and fast indoor courts.
Letná Park, Praha 7. Tel: 233 374 033.

Ice hockey is one of the major sports in the Czech Republic

Food and drink

Czech cuisine has traditionally been strong in the meat department (per capita meat consumption under the Husák regime rose to half a kilo per person per day) and correspondingly weak in vegetables. The heavy dishes come from the heartlands of Bohemia, Moravia and Slovakia. German influence is evident in the various (delicious) sausages and the ubiquitous pickled cabbage. A welcome relief from red meat is provided by the freshwater fish (carp and trout) and increased imports of sea fish.

Nevertheless, the typical national dish remains roast pork with cabbage and dumplings. Dumplings are the real glory of Bohemian cuisine. Of course, visitors to Prague can enjoy pizza, vegetarian, ethnic and international cuisine throughout the capital.

TYPICAL DISHES AND SPECIALITIES
Soups (*polévka*) and entrées (*předkrmy*)

Bramborová polévka: potato soup
Chléb: chewy brown bread
Chlebíčky: open sandwich
Čočková: lentil soup
Fazolová polévka: bean soup
Hovězí vývar: consommé, bouillon
Kulajda: creamy egg and dill soup
Omeleta: omelette
Pražská šunka: Prague ham
Pražská šunka s křenem: Prague ham with horseradish
Pražská šunka s okurkou: Prague ham with gherkins

Smažený sýr: hot fried Edam in breadcrumbs
Tresčí játra: cod's liver
Uzený jazyk: smoked tongue
Vajíčkový salát: egg in mayonnaise

KNEDLÍKY (BOHEMIAN DUMPLINGS)

Dumplings are made from bread, potato dough, soft curd or flour. Usually served as accompaniments to meat dishes, they also come in more sophisticated guises, the best being fruit dumplings. Here is a recipe for fruit dumplings made from potato dough.

Ingredients: 800g boiled potatoes, 10g salt, 2 eggs, 100g semolina, 200g wholemeal flour, a teaspoonful cinnamon, fresh fruit for filling.

Peel potatoes and grate them. Sprinkle with flour, semolina and salt. Make a well in the mixture for the eggs. Knead into dough and form pancakes. Add the fruit, close the mixture into balls and seal them. Place in boiling water and cook for 20 minutes. Remove and sprinkle with cinnamon, breadcrumbs fried in butter, or with poppy seeds and sugar. Melted butter or whipped cream makes a good topping.

Žampióny s vejci:
mushroom with eggs

Main courses
Biftek s vejcem: beef
and eggs
Drštky: tripe
Guláš: goulash
Hovězí: beef
Játra: liver
Kachna: duck
Klobásy: sausages
Knedlíky: dumplings
Krůta: turkey
Kuře: chicken
Skopové: mutton
Smažený řízek: Wiener
Schnitzel
Svíčková na smetaně:
roast loin of beef with
cream sauce
Telecí: veal
Vepřové se zelím: roast
pork with sauerkraut

Vegetables (*zelenina*)
Brambory: potatoes
Červená řepa: beetroot
Cibule: onions
Hranolky: French fries
Kyselé zelí: sauerkraut
Lečo: ratatouille
Obloha: garnish (usually
pickled vegetables)
Okurka: cucumber
Rajčata: tomatoes
Salát: salad
Špenát: spinach
Zelí: cabbage

Fish (*ryby*)
Kapr vařený s máslem:
boiled carp with
melted butter
Pečená štika: roast pike
Platýs: flounder
Pstruh na másle: trout
in melted butter

Dessert (*zákusky*)
Jablečný závin:
apple strudel
Omeleta se zavařeninou:
jam omelette
Palačinky: pancakes
Švestkové knedlíky:
plum dumplings
(always delicious)
Zmrzlina: ice cream

Cheese (*sýr*)
Balkansky sýr: feta cheese
Bryndza: goats' cheese
in brine
Oštěpek: smoked
curd cheese
Tvaroh: curd cheese
Uzený sýr: smoked cheese

Fruit (*ovoce*)
Banán: banana
Borůvky: blueberries
Broskev: peach
Hroznové víno: grapes
Hruška: pear
Jablka: apple
Jahody: strawberries
Kompot: stewed fruit
Maliny: raspberries

Pomeranč: orange
Švestky: plums

WHERE TO EAT
Although the city's
restaurants offer some
of the most atmospheric
medieval and Baroque
interiors in Europe, it
cannot be said that the
food and service have
always lived up to the
mark. However, things
are now noticeably
improving – the variety
and standard of
eateries is on the up-
and-up. Check
www.squaremeal.cz for
good listings and the
latest hotspots, or buy a
copy of *Gourmet*. If your
meal proves to be in
order and if the service
has been halfway
acceptable, a tip of 10 per
cent is usual in top-notch
establishments, a few
crowns elsewhere. Note
that opening times may
change slightly, according
to season.

Reservations are vital
for restaurants, especially
in the high season. The
most popular places may
need to be booked as
much as a week in
advance, although two to

Food and drink

Food and drink

All ready and waiting to welcome customers at a streetside café

beyond the means of all but a minority of Czechs). The price of a glass of wine varies, but 60kč for a quarter litre is not unusual. Beer prices show even greater disparities – anything from around 12kč in a traditional pub to 60kč or more in a popular tourist spot such as U Fleků.

three days is usually adequate. If you have not booked anywhere, you may have to fall back on a beer cellar, café or a fast-food outlet.

Types of eating house

The choice of establishments falls into three main categories: *restaurace* (restaurant), *vinárna* (wine bar or wine cellar) and *pivnice* (beer cellar). The last named usually offers pub food, although that should be regarded in most cases simply as an accompaniment to the serious business of beer consumption.

Creeping gentrification has meant that the distinctions between different types of hostelry have become blurred: in particular, a number of *vinárna*s are now luxury restaurants in all but name.

Because of inflation and changes of ownership, the following guide to prices can only be an indication. Average meal prices in koruna (kč), inclusive of wine, are for a two-course meal for two people.

★ up to 500kč
★★ 501kč to 1,000kč
★★★ 1,001kč to 1,500kč
★★★★ 1,501kč to 3,000kč

Prices can be expected to continue rising, especially in the sort of place largely frequented by foreigners (already

Czech cuisine

Klub Architektů ★

A cellar restaurant offering well-cooked staples such as fried cheese, particularly good with apple and cream sauce, and some fine beers.
Betlemské náměstí 5.
Tel: 224 401 214.
Open: daily
11.30am–midnight.
Metro: Národni třída.

Restaurace Pivovarský Dům ★

A friendly in-house brewery (the staff may be rushed off their feet, but only because the food and beer are satisfyingly good and demand is huge), creatively decorated with paraphernalia associated with the trade.

*Lipova 15, Nové Město,
Prague 2.
Tel: 296 216 666.
Open: daily
11am–11.30pm. Metro:
I P Pavlova.*

Patriot-X ★★

The aim of the Patriot-X
is to breathe new life into
Czech cuisine and revive
some old aristocratic
Bohemian dishes, which
it achieves with
perfection and passion.
You won't eat better
Czech food in the capital
these days.

*V Celnici 3, Nové Město.
Tel: 224 235 158. Open:
daily 10am–midnight.
Metro: Náměstí republiky.*

U Vladaře ★★★

Game and traditional
Czech cuisine, served
with flair and in huge
portions, plus local wines
(fair) and beer
(unbeatable).

*Maltézské náměstí 10
(Malá Strana).
Tel: 222 716 003. Open:
daily noon–midnight.
Metro: Malostranská.
Trams: 12, 20, 22 & 23.*

International cuisine

Pod Křídlem ★★

A well-kept secret
amid the hustle and

bustle of central Prague.
Enjoy affordable
international fare
while people-watching
through the huge
windows or in the more
intimate Art Deco
ambience of the rear
dining room.

*Národní 10, Nové Město.
Tel: 224 951 741. Open:
Mon–Fri 10am–midnight,
Sat & Sun 11.30am–
midnight.*

Nebozízek ★★★

Reached by the funicular
railway on Petřín,
celebrated as much for
the wonderful view as
for the game and
Bohemian cooking.

*Petřínské sady 411.
Tel: 257 315 329.
Open: daily 11am–11pm.
Trams: 6, 9, 12 & 22 to
Újezd, then via railway.*

David ★★★★

Small, exquisite and chic.
Good salad and poultry.

*Tržiště 21. Tel: 257 533
109. Open: daily
11.30am–11pm.
Trams: 12, 20, 22 & 23 to
Malostranské náměstí.*

V Zátiší ★★★★

Nouvelle cuisine comes
to Prague! Now
something of a golden
oldie, the fish and duck

are highly recommended.
*Liliová 1. Tel: 222 221
155. Open: daily noon–
3pm, 5.30pm–midnight.
Metro: Národní třída.*

Fish restaurants

Reykjavík ★★★

Fast-frozen Icelandic fish
that tastes absolutely
fresh: salmon, shrimp,
cod, haddock. Fish soup
is a speciality. Service
excellent; no reservations.

*Karlova 20. Tel: 222 221
218. Open: daily
11am–midnight.
Metro: Staroměstská.*

Rybí Trh ★★★

Superb fresh fish and
seafood and alfresco
dining in summer.

*Týn 5, Staré Město.
Tel: 224 895 447.
Open: daily
11am–midnight.*

Kampa Park ★★★★

Very swanky, elegant
restaurant run by a
Swede, with one of
the best river views in
town.

*Na kampě 8b, Malá
Strana. Tel: 257 532 685.
Open: daily
11.30am–1am.*

Radisson Hotel ★★★★

The superbly renovated
old Alcron hotel.

Food and drink

Probably Prague's top fish restaurant.
Štěpánská 40, Nové Město. Tel: 222 820 000. Open: Mon–Sat 6pm–10.30pm.

Game restaurants
U Svatého Huberta ★★
A traditional restaurant serving fine Bohemian venison, wild boar, forest mushrooms and freshwater fish. Brings a welcome taste of the Czech countryside to central Prague.
Husova 7, Staré Město. Tel: 222 221 706. Open: 11.30am–midnight. Metro: Můstek.
Myslivna ★★★
Traditional game restaurant.
Jagellonská 21, Praha 3. Tel: 222 723 252. Open: daily 11am–11pm. Metro: Flora.

ETHNIC RESTAURANTS
Afghan
Ariana ★
Huge portions of rice, kebabs and salads in the heart of the old town.
Rámová 6, Praha 1. Tel: 222 323 438.

Open: daily 11am–11pm. Metro: Staroměstská.

Chinese
Huang He ★
Off the beaten track, but arguably the best Chinese restaurant in Prague. Hurried, noisy, with delicious grub (booking essential).
Vršovická 1, Vršovice, Praha 10. Tel: 271 746 651. Open: daily 11am–11pm. Trams: 6, 7 & 24 to Nádraži Vršovice.

French
La Provence ★★/★★★
Basement Provençal restaurant (specialities include *lavender crème brulée*) with a raucous bar upstairs and an oyster bar in season.
Štupartská 9, Staré Město. Tel: 224 816 692. Open: daily noon–midnight. Metro: Náměstí Republiky or Můstek.
Vas-y Vas-y ★★
Very relaxing. Great food, good wine.
Pštrossova 8, Praha 1. Tel: 224 930 156. Open: daily 11.30am–midnight. Metro: Karlovo náměstí. Trams: 6, 22 & 23 plus most night trams.

Indian and Pakistani
Jewel of India ★★★
Superb cuisine, an authentic tandoor oven, an extensive and innovative menu, and a library of Indian cookbooks and guide books to browse.
Pařížská 20, Praha 1. Tel: 224 811 010. Open: 6–11pm. Metro: Staroměstská.

Italian
Pizza Coloseum ★
Packed basement pizzeria serving fresh and ample salads, pasta and classic Italian staples. Serves good beer too.
Vodičkova 32, Praha 1. Tel: 224 214 914. Open: daily 11am–midnight (reservations not possible). Metro: Můstek.

Russian
Restaurant Tbilisi ★★★★
Very pricey, good cooking and security-conscious. Look out for the stuffed bear by the door.
Dittrichova 25, Praha 2. Tel: 224 911 508. Open: Mon–Sat 6pm–midnight. Metro: Karlovo náměstí.

Thai

Arzenal ★★★

Artistic with fresh and authentic cuisine. Style gallery and shop.
Valentinská 11, Staré Město. Tel: 224 814 099. Open: daily 10am–midnight.

VEGETARIAN FOOD

Though the situation has improved to some degree over the last decade and a half, vegetarians will still be limited to a few cheese and egg dishes in many restaurants. And don't be surprised to find a slice of ham in your fried cheese or omelette! There are still only a handful of vegetarian restaurants in Prague, although the standard of these is high.

Vegetarian eateries

Country Life ★★

One of the longest-established vegetarian restaurants in town. Grab a tray and help yourself to the appetising, healthy fare on offer. If you enjoy your meal, you can even buy the raw ingredients in the adjoining shop.

Melantrichova 15, Staré Město. Tel: 224 213 366. Open: Mon–Thur 9am–8.30pm, Fri 9am–6.30pm, Sun 11am–8.30pm.

Govinda ★★

Prague's Hare Krishna restaurant where the 100 per cent vegetarian dishes are cheap, simple but incredibly tasty.
Soukenická 27, Staré Město. Tel: 224 813 096. Open: Mon–Fri 11am–5pm.

WHAT TO DRINK

The two major wine-growing areas of former Czechoslovakia are around Břeclav in Southern Moravia and Pezinok in Western Slovakia. Both regions are near enough to Prague for pleasant weekend excursions; these can be a lot of fun (and pretty alcoholic) during the wine harvest season from mid-September to late October. The picturesque Moravian *sklípky* (wine cellars) that border the vineyards offer opportunities for wine-tasting, dancing and eating until you explode.

Neither the Czech lands nor Slovakia can truthfully be described as producing classic wines, but the best of them are pleasantly drinkable. The consensus is that Moravian wine outshines the rest, and many of the Prague cellars specialise in their products. Good wine is also made at Mělník, which is near enough to the capital for a lunch or dinner outing (*see p139*).

Wines

White wine is generally more favoured than the red, and almost invariably drunk within a couple of years of the harvest. *Sauvignon*, which is aromatic with a flavour of ripe peaches, is often an exception to this general rule – the best is said to come from Velké Pavlovice in Moravia. *Ryzlink rýnský*, claimed to be the 'king of wines and the wine of kings', has a bouquet of lime blossom and is good with fish. *Rulandské bílé* is more full-bodied and often likened to a Burgundy. Connoisseurs of Austrian wine will

Food and drink

warm to the *Veltlínské zelené*, the fresh, somewhat acidic *Grüner Veltliner*. Czechs do not mind drinking white wine with roasts, but for this they will probably choose a *Neuburské* (Neuburger) with its slightly smoky taste.

Müller Thurgau is good with fish or veal, while *Silván* is suited to pâté and chicken. A fine Moravian Riesling with limited production is *Bzenecká lipka*, often drunk with grilled meat. Of the reds, *Rulandské červené* has some of the characteristics of a Burgundy, while the velvety *Vavřinecké* wins praise from enthusiasts.

Vinárny and wine bars
Prague has a vast number of 'wine cellars' and cocktail and wine bars. Here are some recommendations:
Šenk Vrbovec ★
At this basic, down-to-earth place, popular with locals, you can enjoy cheap Moravian reds and whites drawn straight from the barrel. Superb location and a real

antidote to Prague's growing number of pretentious, overpriced bars. No food, just fine local wine.
Václavské náměstí 10, Nové Město.
Tel: 723 716 295.
Open: Mon–Sat 10am–11pm, Sun 2–11pm.
U Zlatého Tygra ★
A typical spit-and-sawdust Czech pub of the type more often found in the countryside than in snooty Prague 1. Expect lots of spilt beer and loud pub philosophy, and don't even think of sitting in the place once reserved for writer Bohumil Hrabal.
Husova 17, Staré Město.
Tel: 222 221 111.
Open: daily 3–11pm.
Gargoyle's ★★/★★★
Slick Californian and French cuisine, washed down with a good selection of local and international wines; fine-tasting 'gourmet' menu.
Opatovická 5, Staré Město. Tel: 224 916 047.
Open: 11am–3pm, 5.30pm–midnight.
Metro: Národní třída.
Barock ★★★
Very swanky hang-out with cocktails and sushi.

Pařížska 24, Staré Město.
Tel: 222 329 221.
Open: daily 10am–1am.
Metro: Staroměstská.
Ostroff ★★★
Although not strictly a wine bar, this does have a superb view over the river. The island-based restaurant is high-scale Italian, with correspondingly good wines, and has one of Prague's longest cocktail bars.
Střelecky Ostrov (Sharp-shooters' Island) 336, Staré Město. Tel: 224 919 235. Open: Mon–Fri noon–2pm, 7–11.30pm; Sat 7–11.30pm; Sun 11am–3pm, 7–11.30pm.
Metro: Národní třída.

Pivnice (beer halls)
U Betlémské Kaple ★
Bohumil Hrabal wrote lyrically about the *12° prazdroj* beer served here 'with its marvellous head . . . like whipped cream'. The pub is good value and offers tasty food.
Betlémské náměstí 2.
Tel: 222 221 639.
Open: daily 11am–11pm.
Metro: Národní třída.
Novoměstský pivovar ★★
Prague's most central

BEER

In the dozens of alehouses in Prague you will come across a wide range of beers, food and prices. Most pubs are tied to the products of one brewery – Pilsner Urquell, or Budvar. Often the beers will be from one of the breweries in Prague itself.

microbrewery, where a warren of underground cellars fills every evening with drinkers and diners enjoying tankards of unfiltered ale and huge portions of stodgy Bohemian fare.
Vodičkova 20, Nové Město. Tel: 222 232 448. Open: Mon–Fri 10am–11.30pm, Sat 11.30am–11.30pm, Sun noon–10pm. Trams: 3, 9, 14 & 24 to Vodičkova.

U Fleků ★★
The sweetish black ale, made since 1843 to a Bavarian recipe, is brewed and sold only on the premises of this five-centuries-old brewery. It is best to sit in the garden – brimming mugs arrive automatically, and there are normally one or two hot dishes of the day to choose from.

Křemencova 11. Tel: 224 934 019. Open: daily 9am–11pm. Metro: Karlovo náměstí.

U Kalicha (The Chalice) ★★
This was The Good Soldier Švejk's favourite watering hole; the place is very touristy, but the food and Pilsner are excellent. Reservations advisable.
Na bojišti 12. Tel: 296 189 600. Open: 11am–11pm. Metro: I P Pavlova.

Kavárny (cafés)

Café Evropa ★
Indifferent menu but superb Art Nouveau interior.
Václavske náměstí 29. Tel: 224 228 117. Open: daily 9am–11.30pm. Metro: Muzeum or Můstek.

Café Savoy ★
Enjoy the painted neo-Renaissance ceiling and Viennese interior of this beautifully restored café.
Vitězná 5, Praha 5. Tel: 257 311 562. Open: Mon–Fri 8am–10.30pm, Sat & Sun 9am–10.30pm. Trams: 9 & 22 to Újezd.

Grand Café Praha ★
A reasonably priced Old Town Square café with a superb view of the astronomical clock.
Staroměstské náměsti 22. Tel: 221 632 522. Open: 8am–midnight.

Kavárna Lucerna ★
Enjoy a Turkish coffee at this piano bar on the first floor of the Lucerna Palace, surrounded by untouched Art Nouveau décor and in the company of Czechs waiting for the cinema to begin.
Lucerna Palace, Štěpánská 61, Nové Město. Open: Mon–Sat 10am–1am, Sun 10am–11pm. Metro: Muzeum or Můstek.

Obecní Dům ★ (The Municipal House)
Another fine Art Nouveau interior. A pleasant place to write your postcards home, and nosh coffee and cakes.
Náměstí Republiky 5. Tel: 222 002 763. Open: 7.30am–11pm. Metro: Náměstí Republiky.

Slavia ★
The famous writers' (and dissidents') Art Deco café, but service is slow.
Národní 1. Tel: 224 218 493. Open: daily 8am–11pm. Trams: 6, 9, 18, 22 & 23 to Národní Divadlo.

Beer culture

Beer, to the true-born Czech, is not so much a drink as a way of life. It is nearly impossible to drink an unpalatable brew in Prague, and aficionados of brands are as passionately divided in their enthusiasm as the supporters of the city's two football clubs.

The distinctive, bottom-fermented *Plzeňský prazdroj* (Pilsner Urquell) was first produced in the Bohemian town of Plzeň in 1842. Its great rival is Budvar from *České Budějovice* (Budweis). Flavoured with the hand-picked 'red' hops of Bohemia, the secret of these tipples (as of Scotch whisky) is the soft water used in the brewing. A high carbon dioxide content ensures a fine, flowery head: to test the quality, Praguers stand a matchstick in the foam. The contents are satisfactory if it stays erect for at least ten seconds. Mercifully, Czech breweries have stuck to traditional ingredients and methods, which means the beer-drinker is spared the characterless chemical fizz cynically foisted on Western consumers.

The seriousness of these drinking matters may be seen from the founding of a Party for the Friends of Beer after the Velvet Revolution. Its members appointed themselves guardians of beer quality in the capital, which naturally involved them in the onerous duties of rigorous testing and consumption. Unfortunately, the party has been unable to prevent a scandalous rise in prices, although connoisseurs will whisper to each other the names of a few places that still serve pils at 20kč or less. The discovery that one well-known hostelry had raised its prices to an unheard-of 50kč per glass provoked national outrage. A country whose ex-president once worked as a brewery hand does not take kindly to profiteering with a commodity so close to a Czech's heart.

Budvar is a great rival to Pilsner

In Prague, beer is a way of life

Hotels and accommodation

Prague today offers a better and more appealing choice of rooms than in the past, although prices are barely different from those in Berlin or Paris. Some 'state-of-the-art' modern hotels have also opened, in addition to an appealing collection of pensions.

Prices

Most hotels have now switched to the Western star system of grading, although it will be some time before service and accommodation fully meet Western standards. In general, hotels are still expensive for what they offer.

Shabby chic at the Evropa

Private accommodation now provides a pleasant and economic alternative.

The following is an indication of what one might expect to pay for a double hotel room in Prague at the time of writing. Inflation and renovation costs will certainly increase prices. Breakfast is not always included, and hotels in the bottom two categories may have rooms without en-suite bathrooms. Below five-star, the star rating requires flexible interpretation. Hotel bills must be paid in Czech koruna regardless of which currency the hotel lists its prices in (often euros).

★   up to 1,500kč
★★   1,500–2,999kč
★★★   3,000–4,999kč
★★★★   5,000–7,999kč
★★★★★ 8,000kč or above

Private accommodation is usually better value than a modest hotel, although in some cases facilities may have to be with a family; in others, the hospitality may overwhelm the fainthearted. Prices start at around 400kč per person. Rooms in seasonally rented college dormitories are cheaper, though they will still cost about 280–500kč per person. In fact, many new hostels in Prague offer better facilities than a three-star pension.

Location

The hotels around the core of old Prague (Staré Město, Nové Město, Malá Strana) are almost all expensive. A few new luxury hotels have been built further out, but all of them have good connections to the centre. The mix of residential and commercial properties in the old heart of the city means that it is usually possible to find private accommodation near the centre.

Motels and camping sites are just outside the city. However, access by bus or tram to the centre of town should be reasonably easy.

Booking

Trying to book a hotel directly can be a frustrating business and is not always reliable. Try the following websites for listings, and online booking for a huge list of hotels, pensions, hostels and rooms for rent, to suit all budgets (*www.pis.cz*, *www.ave.cz* and *www.hostelworld.com*).

Travellers may still sometimes be told that Prague is 'fully booked' – apparently for a whole season. This could be technically true, in the sense that many of the city's hotels that are in the middle to upper price ranges are often block-booked a year ahead by package tour operators. However, there will still be accommodation available elsewhere.

Reaching for the skies, the Forum Hotel in Vyšehrad

Booking agencies in Prague

If you have arrived in Prague without a booking (or wish to change the hotel you have), there are now a lot of agencies that can help you find accommodation. You will also be offered rooms to rent by individuals at the Main Railway Station and at Holešovice Railway Station. Clearly, it is essential to check that the rooms are centrally located, or close to public transport – but you rent these at your own risk. AVE has an excellent accommodation service at both stations. Other agencies include:

Agentura STOP CITY Pensions, rooms and hotels (*www.stopcity.com*).

Euroagentur Online hotel bookings and other tourist services (*www.euroagentur.com*).

Hotels Czech Hotels and other accommodation in the Czech Republic (*www.hotelsczech.com*).

Prague Bed and Breakfast Hotels, studios and apartments (*www.praguebedandbreakfast.com*).

Luxury hotels

The shortage of hotel beds at the luxury end of the market was already being remedied under the Communist regime, with an eye to the foreign business traveller. Among the luxury hotels are the **Marriott** (*tel: 222 888 888*), the **Four Seasons** (*tel: 221 427 000*) and the **Radisson SAS Hotel Praha** (*tel: 222 820 000*) – the last in a superbly renovated Art Deco building.

You could also try the following: the **Hotel Josef** (*tel: 221 700 111*), a

A formal welcome at Hotel Atrium

boutique hotel near the Jewish Quarter; **Ventana** (*tel: 221 776 600*), a new, up-market hotel, with a great location near the Old Town Square; **Carlo IV** (*tel: 224 593 111*) in the New Town near the main railway station; **Questenberk** (*tel: 220 407 600*), in a historical setting near Prague Castle, four-star equivalent; **Palace Hotel** (*tel: 224 093 111*), five-star luxury in the heart of the New Town; and **Castle Steps** (*tel: 800 227 853*), in Malá Strana, which gets rave reviews from travellers.

Traditional hotels

Sadly, only a few of the old-style hotels have retained real character and authentic décor. The best preserved of the Art Nouveau hotels are the truly shabby **Evropa** (*tel: 224 228 215*) and the Art Nouveau **Pařiž** (*tel: 222 195 666*), but they are difficult to book. An atmospheric little hotel is **U Tří Pštrosů** (*tel: 257 288 888*), in a Renaissance house at the Malá Strana end of Charles Bridge. There are a number of other traditional hotels that tend to be clustered round the centre: the friendly **Casa Marcello** (*tel: 222 311 230*), **Kampa** (*tel: 257 404 200*) and **Esplanade** (*tel: 224 501 111*) are all in the city centre.

Botels

Staying on the River Vltava sounds appealing, but the reality may be otherwise. There are three 'botels'; the **Admirál** (*tel: 257 321 302*) is the best of the bunch.

Pensions/small hotels

Pensions and cheaper modern hotels are mostly located some way from the centre. Many can be found in Prague 6 and 2. A great affordable hotel is the ex-police complex where former President Václav Havel was imprisoned: **Hotel Cloister Inn**, *Konviktska 14, Praha 1, tel: 224 211 020; www.cloister-inn.com.*
Other options include **Hotel Antik** (*tel: 222 322 288*) in the old town and **Pension u Meduídků** (*tel: 224 211 916*) just off Národní Trída.

Youth hostels

For bookings use *www.hostelworld.com* to check out the great selection of hostels and pensions in Prague. Or try **Travellers Hostel**, *Dlouha 33, Praha 1. Tel: 224 826 662. www.travellers.cz*

A taste of classic Prague at the Palace Hotel in the New Town

On business

Since the Czech Republic's entry into the European Union in 2004, the business community in Prague has become increasingly cosmopolitan. Most former state organisations have been privatised, or are adapting themselves to life in a competitive market environment. Bohemia and Moravia offer the most attractive investment possibilities for the future. Investors continue to be attracted in droves. (For more information, see *www.czechinvest.com*)

Business hours

Most offices start at 9am and close at 5pm. Ministries in Prague are open 8am–4pm, Monday to Friday. Banks are generally open 8am–4pm, Monday to Friday, but some in the city centre have longer hours and close for an hour at lunchtime.

Conference centres and trade fairs

Conferences are most prominently held at the Prague Congress Centre (or KCP), which hosted the World Bank/IMF conference in 2000 with considerable aplomb. Trade fairs are held at the main Prague venue: the Výstaviště complex in Holešovice, Prague 7 (metro line C to Nádraží Holešovice, trams 5, 12 and 17 to Výstaviště). Brno is the major trade fair city. Contact **BVV** (*tel: 541 151 111* or *www.bvv.cz*) for details.

Courier

International courier services – **DHL** (*tel: 800 103 000, www.dhl.cz*); local 24-hour messenger services by **Messenger** (*tel: 220 400 000, www.messenger.cz*). Try local listings for other courier agencies (*www.praguepost.com*).

Etiquette

Wearing a suit is almost obligatory for the businessman here, so a more casual mode of dress can be taken as implying lack of seriousness. Czechs are punctilious in matters of formal courtesy, always shaking hands on meeting and at leave-taking.

Internet access

Major hotels offer high-speed internet access to guests, and there are cyber-cafés popping up everywhere. Prague has plans to extend a free wi-fi network, currently only available in certain districts, to the rest of the city.

Money

The *Prague Post* is a weekly newspaper, published on Wednesdays. It has commerce-oriented articles in its finance section, and gives the current exchange rates.

The Czech koruna (crown) (kč) is fully convertible, although the Czech Republic hopes to join the euro zone in 2012.

Office supplies

These are really ubiquitous. Try Tesco, or any of the family-run *papírnictvís*. **Activa** (*www.activa.cz*) offers stationery and equipment online.

Photocopying

Possibly the best Prague copy service is **C-Copy Centrum**, on Opletalova 22 (*tel: 224 212 110*), which features pick-up and delivery services. Otherwise, try the 24-hour copy shop, **Copy General** (*Senovážné nám. 26, tel: 224 230 020*).

Secretarial services

Regus (*www.regus.com*) offers full office and secretarial services to those new to the scene (*Klimentská 46, Nové Město, tel: 222 191 111*).

There are also ample human resources and recruitment agencies, only too eager to offer their assistance.

Check the *Prague Book of Lists*, published by the *Prague Post* (*www.praguepost.com*), for company listings, or try *Czech Business Weekly* (*www.cbw.cz*).

Translation

Organisations offering interpreting services include:

ArtLingua: *Myslíkova 6.*
Tel: 224 918 058; fax: 224 921 715.
www.artlingua.cz
Finist: Interpretation and translation.
Štěpánská 16, Praha 1,
Tel: 296 226 950.
www.finist.cz
Skřívánek: Interpretation and translation services.
Washingtonova 17, Praha 1.
Tel: 221 666 630.
www.skrivanek.cz

Telefax/telegram/telephone

At the Main Post Office at Jindřiška 14 (open 24 hours). *See also p185.*

Ministries in Prague are only open on weekdays

Practical guide

Arriving
Formalities
A valid passport and, in the case of travellers from South Africa, a visa (obtained in country of residence and valid for three months) are required. See *www.mvcr.cz* for visa information.

By air
Ruzyně Airport is 20km (12 miles) west of the city. **CEDAZ** minibus travels from Náměstí Republiky to the airport every half-hour from 6am–11pm. Alternatively, CEDAZ can arrange pick-up at your hotel (*tel: 220 114 296*). Airport taxis will drop you in central Prague for about 500kč, and they operate until late evening. The airport (flight enquiry number *220 113 314*) has facilities for telephone, currency exchange (24 hours), car rental desks and an accommodation bureau.

Prague is served by several European carriers including Aer Lingus (*www.flyaerlingus.com*), British Airways (*www.britishairways.com*), BMI Baby (*www.flybmi.com*), Czech Airlines (*www.csa.cz*), easyJet (*www.easyjet.com*), and Jet2 (*www.jet2.com*).

By rail
From London to Prague takes 18 to 24 hours, according to route. Information from **Raileurope Travel Centre**, *178*

A view over the rooftops of Prague

Practical guide

Piccadilly, London W1 (opposite the Royal Academy of Arts), *tel: 08448 484 064; www.raileurope.co.uk*

Timetables of Czech national and international services can be found in the *Thomas Cook European Timetable*, available from branches of Thomas Cook in the UK, or telephone *01733 416477*. Another great site is *www.vlak-bus.cz*, which gives bus and train schedules from/to the Czech Republic.

Trains arrive in Prague at Hlavní nádraží (Central Railway Station), or further out at the Nádraží Praha Holešovice. Both are on the Metro (line C). InterRail cards are valid for travel in the Czech Republic.

By road

The Czech Republic has border crossings with Germany, Poland, the Slovak Republic and Austria. All except a few on minor roads are open 24 hours.

Camping

For campsites in the Czech Republic see *www.czech-camping.com*

Camp Dana Troja

For simple tents and caravans. Hot showers, toilet facilities, etc. Very cheap. *Trojska 129, Praha 7, tel: 283 850 482; www.volny.cz/campdana. Metro: Holešovice.*

Camping Trio Camp

A few kilometres off the D-E55 highway to the north of Prague, 9km (5½ miles) from the centre. Toilet facilities and showers, micromarket, snack bar. For tents and caravans. Very cheap.

Ústecká ulice, Praha 8 – Dolní Chabry, tel: 283 850 793; www.triocamp.cz

Campsite Convoy

Císařská Louka 599, Smíchov, Praha 5, tel: 257 318 681; www.volny.cz/convoy

Children

Children under six travel free on the Metro, tram and bus networks; six- to 15-year-olds pay half fare. Under-fives travel free on Czech national rail; five- to ten-year-olds pay half fare. There is a childcare clinic at the hospital complex at **Na Homolce**, *Roentgenova 2, Smíchov, Praha 5 (tel: 257 272 144)*, as well as private, 'Western-style' clinics (*see also* Health), or **Poliklinika na Národní**, *Národní, 3rd floor (tel: 222 075 120)*.

Climate

See p8.

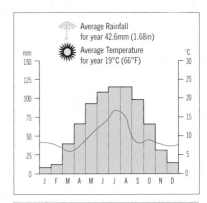

WEATHER CONVERSION CHART

25.4mm = 1 inch

°F = 1.8 × °C + 32

Crime

Petty crime is still fairly frequent. Trams on tourist routes, such as Nos 22 and 23, are worked by pickpocketing gangs. Don't leave valuables inside your vehicle; use your hotel safe. Report any crime in person at the main police station at *Bartolomějská 6, Staré Město, Praha 1*. The emergency telephone number for the police is *tel: 158*.

Keep a photocopy handy of your passport details, credit card numbers and the like, in case of theft.

Customs regulations

From outside the EU it is permissible to bring into the Czech Republic free of duty all personal effects plus 200 cigarettes, two litres of wine, one litre of spirits and 50g of perfume. Money can be exported. Only non-EU residents can claim tax refund (VAT refund) for items costing more than 2,000kč. *See www.globalrefund.com*

Driving

Driving in the centre of Prague is not easy, and it is easy to stray into zones restricted to public transport and permit holders (as in Wenceslas Square). On-the-spot fines are levied. If you are towed away, *tel: 158* to find out where your car is held.

Breakdown

The 'Yellow Angels' provide a breakdown service (*tel: 1230/1240*). It is advisable to have comprehensive insurance to cover all eventualities and

A woman has her portrait drawn

repatriation. For the 24-hour repair service for foreign cars, *tel: 251 613 835*.

Car hire

You must be over 21, have a valid licence, and have been driving for at least a year. ID and a credit card are required when you reserve a car. **Alimex** (*tel: 233 350 001; www.alimexcr.cz*) is cheaper than most.

Documents and insurance

Most national driving licences are valid, but an International Driving Licence is advisable for Australian and New Zealand drivers. Take the vehicle's registration document. It is also obligatory to carry a first-aid kit, a red warning triangle, and replacement light bulbs – and to display a national identification sticker.

Fuel

Petrol (*benzín*) is available as *super* (leaded 96 octane), *special* (leaded 91 octane), *natural* (unleaded 95 octane),

super plus (unleaded 98 octane), and
nafta (diesel).

Parking

Most parking around the centre is for
residents only. Whenever possible, park
on the outskirts of the city and
continue your journey by public
transport, or use the multistorey car
parks in the centre.

Traffic regulations

Drive on the right. Seatbelts are
obligatory, and children under 12 must
travel in the back. All vehicles must
have their headlights switched on, day
and night, year round. There is zero
tolerance for driving under the
influence of alcohol. Overtaking trams
is forbidden at passenger stops (unless
there is a passenger island at the stop).
Trams have right of way – be alert
when crossing tram lines. Speed limits
are 130kph on motorways, 90kph on
roads, 50kph in built-up areas, and
30kph at level crossings (many have no
barriers). All accidents must be
reported to the police (*tel: 158*).

Electricity

220 volts, 50 cycle AC. Standard
continental adaptors are suitable.
Visitors with appliances that require
100/120 volts will need a voltage
transformer.

Embassies

Australia *Klimentská 10, Praha 1.
Tel: 296 578 350.*

CONVERSION TABLE

FROM	TO	MULTIPLY BY
Inches	Centimetres	2.54
Feet	Metres	0.3048
Yards	Metres	0.9144
Miles	Kilometres	1.6090
Acres	Hectares	0.4047
Gallons	Litres	4.5460
Ounces	Grams	28.35
Pounds	Grams	453.6
Pounds	Kilograms	0.4536
Tons	Tonnes	1.0160

To convert back, for example from
centimetres to inches, divide by the number
in the third column.

MEN'S SUITS

UK	36	38	40	42	44	46	48
Prague & Rest of Europe	46	48	50	52	54	56	58
USA	36	38	40	42	44	46	48

DRESS SIZES

UK	8	10	12	14	16	18
France	36	38	40	42	44	46
Italy	38	40	42	44	46	48
Prague & Rest of Europe	34	36	38	40	42	44
USA	6	8	10	12	14	16

MEN'S SHIRTS

UK	14	14.5	15	15.5	16	16.5	17
Prague & Rest of Europe	36	37	38	39/40	41	42	43
USA	14	14.5	15	15.5	16	16.5	17

MEN'S SHOES

UK	7	7.5	8.5	9.5	10.5	11
Prague & Rest of Europe	41	42	43	44	45	46
USA	8	8.5	9.5	10.5	11.5	12

WOMEN'S SHOES

UK	4.5	5	5.5	6	6.5	7
Prague & Rest of Europe	38	38	39	39	40	41
USA	6	6.5	7	7.5	8	8.5

Canada *Muchova 6, Hradčany, Praha 6.*
Tel: 272 101 800.
UK *Thunovská 14, Malá Strana.*
Tel: 257 402 111.
USA *Tržiště 15, Malá Strana.*
Tel: 257 022 000.

Emergency telephone numbers
Ambulance *Tel: 155.*
Chemist (24-hour) *Lékárna Palackého,*
Palackého 5, Praha 1 (tel: 224 946 982).
Lékárna U svaté Ludmily, Belgická 37,
Prague 2 (tel: 224 237 207).
Dentist *Palackého 5, Nové Město. Tel:*
224 946 981. Open: Mon–Fri 7am–7pm,
Sat–Sun 24 hours.
Doctor (emergency service) *Tel: 155.*
Fire brigade *Tel: 150.*
First aid *Tel: 155.*
General information *Tel: 12 444.*
Municipal police *Tel: 156.*
Police *Tel: 158.*
Yellow Angels (car breakdown)
Tel: 1230/1240.

Health
Emergency treatment is free. A
reciprocal health care agreement
exists between the UK and the Czech
Republic which covers most, but not
all, eventualities. For this you must
obtain a European Health Insurance
Card before you travel. The card is
available from *www.ehic.org.uk*, by
phoning *0845 605 2030*, or from post
offices. US passport holders must pay
for treatment. If you need attention,
apply to the **Unicare 24-hour call**
service (*Na dlouhém lánu 11, Praha 6.*

Tel: 235 356 553). For private
treatment, you can attend the
Diplomatic Health Centre at *Na*
Homolce, Roentgenova 2, Praha 5 –
Smíchov (tel: 257 272 146; open:
Mon–Fri 7.30am–4pm). A deposit of at
least 1,000kč will be required.

Insurance
You should take out personal travel
insurance from your travel agent, tour
operator or insurance company. It
should give adequate cover for medical
expenses, loss or theft, repatriation,
personal liability, third-party motor
insurance (but liability arising from
motor accidents is not usually
included) and cancellation expenses.
Always read the conditions, and make
sure the amount of cover is adequate.

If you hire a car, collision insurance
(often called collision damage waiver
or CDW) is usually compulsory and
charged by the hirer, but it may be as
much as 50 per cent of the hiring fee.
Check with your own motor insurers
before you leave, as you may already
be covered for CDW on overseas hires
by your normal policy. Neither CDW
nor your personal travel insurance will
protect you from liability arising out of
an accident in a hire car, for example, if
you damage another vehicle or injure
someone. If you are likely to hire a car
you should obtain such extra cover,
preferably from your travel agent or
other insurer before departure.

If you are taking your own motor
vehicle on holiday, check with your

Language

Czech sounds and looks daunting, but English is increasingly widespread, particularly among the younger generation; most older people speak some German.

PRONUNCIATION

The stress is always on the first syllable of a word.

Vowel sounds

a like the English 'u' in 'up'.
á as in 'rather'.
e as in 'get'.
é similar to 'ai' in 'hair'.
ě like 'ye' as in 'yes'.
i as in 'sit'.
í or ý as in 'meat'.
o as in 'hot'.
ó as in 'claw'.
u as in 'book'.
ů or ú as in 'cool'.

Diphthongs

au as in 'now'.
ou as in 'oh'.

Consonants

Consonants are the same as in English, with the following exceptions:
c as in 'oats'.
č as in 'chess'.
j as in 'you'.
ch as in Scottish 'loch'.
r like English, but rolled.
ř rolled and combined with zh sound in 'pleasure'.
š as in 'she'.
ž like the zh sound in 'pleasure'.
d, t and n, if followed by i or í, become dyi, tyi and nyi.

NUMBERS			
1	jeden	**6**	šest
2	dva	**7**	sedm
3	tří	**8**	osm
4	čtyří	**9**	devět
5	pět	**10**	deset

BASIC PHRASES					
yes	ano	**small**	malý	**cheap**	levný
no	ne	**large**	velký	**near**	blízko
please/		**quickly**	rychle	**far**	daleko
you're		**slowly**	pomalu	**day**	den
welcome	prosím	**cold**	studený	**week**	týden
thank you	děkuji	**hot**	horký	**month**	měsíc
bon appetit	dobrou chut	**left**	nalevo	**year**	rok
hello	ahoj	**right**	napravo		
goodbye	na shledanou	**straight**		**DAYS OF**	
good		**ahead**	přímo	**THE WEEK**	
morning	dobré ráno	**where?**	kde?	**Monday**	pondělí
good day	dobrý den	**when?**	kdy?	**Tuesday**	úterý
good		**why?**	proč?	**Wednesday**	středa
evening	dobrý večer	**open**	otevřeno	**Thursday**	čtvrtek
good night	dobrou noc	**closed**	zavřeno	**Friday**	pátek
		how much?	kolik?	**Saturday**	sobota
		expensive	drahý	**Sunday**	neděle

motoring insurers on your cover. A Green Card is recommended. It is possible to buy packages providing extra cover for breakdowns and accidents.

Internet access
See p176.

Lost property
Apply to *Karolíny Svetle 5, Staré Město (tel: 224 235 085).*

Maps
Tourist Information Offices (*see p188*) and Chequepoint Exchange kiosks issue free street plans. Locally produced Kartografie Praha maps (1:20,000) are recommended.

Media
Prague has several English-language papers: the weekly *Prague Post* has listings, restaurant reviews and other information. It can be bought at newsstands around the centre. Radio 1 (91.9MHz) has a news bulletin in English at 3.30pm on weekdays. Cable TV is widespread, so viewers can access international channels such as CNN and BBC World.

Money matters
The Czech unit of currency is the koruna (Czech crown, abbreviated to kč). It is divided into 100 haléř (hellers). There are 50 heller, 1, 2, 5, 10 and 20kč coins, and 20, 50, 100, 200, 500, 1,000, 2,000 and 5,000kč notes.

Changing money
Usual banking hours are 8am–4pm, Monday to Friday. The airport exchange desk is open 24 hours. Many exchange kiosks charge high commission, and some indulge in suspect practices. For better value go to one of the banks, although they have long queues in high season.

The **Živnostenská Banka** (*Na příkopě* 20) is unbureaucratic, light on charges and open from 8am to 6pm Monday to Friday, and 8am to noon on Saturday. Traveller's cheques are widely accepted at banks and exchange counters if issued by a well-known bank. US dollar cheques are recommended, although cheques denominated in major European currencies are accepted. Many hotels, shops and restaurants in tourist areas will accept traveller's cheques in lieu of cash, or euros at the going rate.

If you need to transfer money quickly, you can use the MoneyGram[SM] Money Transfer service. For more details in the UK, go to *www.moneygram.com*

Credit cards
Credit cards can be used to obtain cash advances from banks and the multitude of cash machines, and are also accepted in most shops and restaurants.
AmEx: *Tel: 222 800 111.*
Diners: *Tel: 267 197 450.*
MasterCard/EuroCard/Visa: *Tel: 272 771 111.*

Opening hours
Banks *See p176.*

Tram 22 runs from the New Town to the castle

Department stores and food shops

9am–6pm, Saturday 9am–noon. Some shops, such as supermarkets, may have longer hours.

Galleries and museums Tuesday to Sunday 10am–5pm (in some cases 6pm or 7pm). All the sights comprising the Jewish Museum in Josefov are closed on Saturdays.

Police

Look for *Policie*. The State Police can be reached in emergencies by dialling *158*. For visa extensions and residence permits, go to *Olšanská 2, Prague 3 (open: Monday to Thursday 7.30–11.30am, noon–4.30pm, 5–7pm).* Be prepared to wait for several hours in utter confusion.

Post offices

The **Central Post Office** and Poste Restante are at *Jindřišská 14, Prague 1 (tel: 221 131 111; www.cpost.cz).* Open 2am–midnight. Stamps and phone cards can be purchased here and from newsagents/tobacconists.

Public holidays

1 January – New Year's Day
Easter Monday – Variable
1 May – Labour Day
8 May – VE Day
5 July – Day of Slav Missionaries Cyril and Methodius
6 July – Jan Hus State Holiday
28 September – St Wenceslas Day
28 October – Independence Day
17 November – Battle for Freedom and Democracy Day, Day of Students
24–26 December – Christmas.

Public transport

Public transport (*see pp26–7*) is relatively cheap and efficient. Separate tickets are not required for each part of a journey involving changes. The Three-, Seven- and 15-Day Passes are valid for all public transport.

The Three-Day Prague Card combines a travel pass with free entry to major sights and some museums. (Apply at **Čedok**, *Na příkopě 18*, **Pragotur**, *Arbesovo Náměstí 4*, or **American Express**, *Václavské náměstí 56. www.praguecard.biz*)

Public transport operates generally between 5am and midnight. Night trams, covering most of central Prague, all stop at Lazarská, close to Wenceslas Square. They leave every 40 minutes between 11.30pm and 4.30am.

Central Bus Station: *Křižíkova 4. For timetable information, tel: 900 144 444; Metro: Florenc.*

English-speaking taxis can be called on *tel: 222 333 222.*

Outside Prague

The rail network connects Prague with many other towns in the Czech Republic, with Germany and with Eastern European cities. For further details and timetables, consult the *Thomas Cook European Timetable*, available from Thomas Cook branches in the UK, or call *01733 416477*. Alternatively, try *www.vlak-bus.cz*

Religious worship

Mass and confession in English are held at St Joseph's Church (Josefská, Malá Strana) every Sunday. Other services for different faiths are also offered. Consult *www.praguepost.com* for listings.

Student and youth travel

GTS International offers plane, train and bus tickets for students, teachers and under-26s. Under-26, ISIC (International Student Identity Card) and ITIC (International Teacher Identity Card) cards are issued here as well. *Ve Smečkach 33, Praha 1. Tel: 222 119 700.*

Sustainable tourism

Thomas Cook is a strong advocate of ethical and fairly traded tourism and believes that the travel experience should be as good for the places visited as it is for the people who visit them. That's why we firmly support The Travel Foundation, a charity that develops solutions to help improve and protect holiday destinations, their environment, traditions and

Prague metro

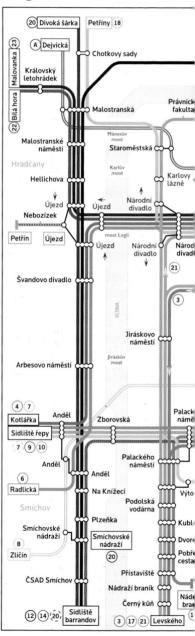

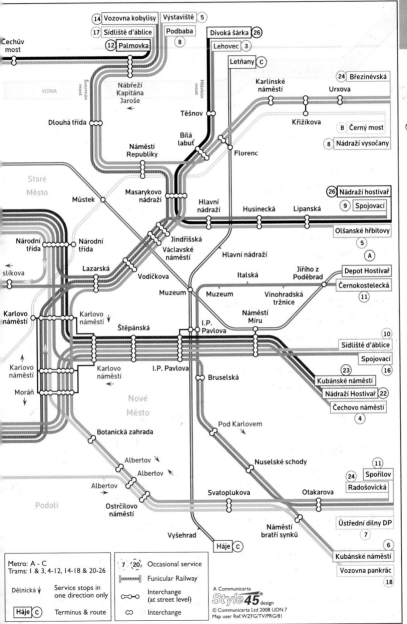

Transport map legend:

Metro: A - C
Trams: 1 & 3, 4-12, 14-18 & 20-26

Dělnická ↓ — Service stops in one direction only

Háje C — Terminus & route

7 (20) — Occasional service

Funicular Railway

∞—∞ — Interchange (at street level)

∞ — Interchange

A Communicarta
Style 45 design
© Communicarta Ltd 2008 UDN.7
Map user Ref:WZFG/TV/PRG/81

culture. To find out what you can do to make a positive difference to the places you travel to and the people who live there, please visit *www.thetravelfoundation.org.uk*

Telephones

All telephone numbers, except service numbers, now have nine digits. The international code for the Czech Republic is *420*.

Modern phone booths that accept telephone cards and coins can be found all over Prague. Most give instructions in English for making international calls. Call the English-speaking operator on *0135*.

Time

The Czech Republic follows Central European Time which is Greenwich Mean Time + 1 hour, or US Eastern Standard Time + 7 hours. Between March and late September clocks are advanced 1 hour (GMT + 2 hours).

Toilets

Scarce, but metro stations quite often have one. The signs are WC or *Muži* (men) and *Ženy* (women). You will usually have to pay 3–5kč.

Tourist information

The **Prague Information Service** (PIS) has its main office at Staroměstské náměstí 1, in the Town Hall Building under the astronomical clock. *Tel: 236 002 562. www.pis.cz. Open: Mon–Fri 9am–6pm, Sat & Sun*

9am–5.30pm, and an hour later in high season. There are other offices at the Mostecká Tower on the west end of the Charles Bridge (at Rytířskí 31) and at Hlavní nádraží (Central Railway Station). For general information, *tel: 221 714 444.*

Travellers with disabilities

Prague is becoming more user-friendly for travellers with disabilities. It is worth contacting the **Association of Disabled People**, *Praha 8, Karlinské nám (tel: 224 816 997, ext 238).* For a list of wheelchair-friendly restaurants, hotels, museums, etc, try *www.allpraha.com*

Obecní dům (Municipal House)

Index

Acknowledgements

Thomas Cook wishes to thank the photographers, picture libraries and other organisations for the loan of the photographs reproduced in this book, to whom copyright in the photographs belongs.

BIGSTOCKPHOTO 115 (Pierrette Guertin); 127 (Sitha Suppalertpisit)
CAROLYN ZUKOWSKI 170, 171
CAROLINE JONES 147
GETTY IMAGES 17
HELENA ZUKOWSKI 18, 21, 23, 59, 65, 67, 79, 80, 93b, 159, 164
JON SMITH 110, 111, 157
LUBOMIR STIBUREK 5, 13, 16, 43, 72, 119, 123, 125, 146
MARC DI DUCA 20, 40, 149, 151, 172, 177, 178, 185
MUCHA MUSEUM 99
MUSEUM OF COMMUNISM 101
PICTURES COLOUR LIBRARY 155
RANDA BISHOP 22, 23, 52, 175
WIKIMEDIA COMMONS 12 (Ales Tovosky); 38; 49 (Prazak); 84; 103 (Che); 8, 188 (Hans Peter Schaefer)
WORLD PICTURES 1, 53, 76
WWW.FLICKR.COM 29, 139 (Julia); 161 (David Watterson)
The remaining pictures are held in the AA PHOTO LIBRARY and were taken by JON WYAND, with the exception of pages 39, 64, 69, 75, 77, 93a, 97, 107 and 117, which were taken by ANTONY SOUTER

For CAMBRIDGE PUBLISHING MANAGEMENT LTD:
Project editor: Robert Wilkinson
Proofreader: Janet McCann
Indexer: Karolin Thomas
Typesetter: Paul Queripel

SEND YOUR THOUGHTS TO
BOOKS@THOMASCOOK.COM

We're committed to providing the very best up-to-date information in our travel guides and constantly strive to make them as useful as they can be. You can help us to improve future editions by letting us have your feedback. If you've made a wonderful discovery on your travels that we don't already feature, if you'd like to inform us about recent changes to anything that we do include, or if you simply want to let us know your thoughts about this guidebook and how we can make it even better – we'd love to hear from you.

Send us ideas, discoveries and recommendations today and then look out for your valuable input in the next edition of this title.

Emails to the above address, or letters to Travellers Series Editor, Thomas Cook Publishing, PO Box 227, Unit 9, Coningsby Road, Peterborough PE3 8SB, UK.

Please don't forget to let us know which title your feedback refers to!